40 Checklists for Managers and Team Leaders

10 Checklists for Managers and Team Leaders

40 Checklists for Managers and Team Leaders

Ian MacKay

Gower

Published by
Gower Publishing Limited
Gower House
Croft Road
Aldershot
Hampshire GU11 3HR
England

Gower
Old Post Road
Brookfield
Vermont 05036
USA

British Library Cataloguing in Publication Data
Mackay, Ian
    40 checklists for managers and team leaders
    1. Management   2. Executives
    I. Title   II. Forty checklists for managers and team leaders
    658.4

ISBN 0 566 07984 4

Phototypeset in New Baskerville by Intype London Ltd and printed in Great Britain by Hartnolls Limited, Bodmin.

Contents

Contents

List of figures

Publisher's note

The late Ian MacKay began compiling checklists in the 1970s as part of his work as a lecturer in human resource management and development. They reflect his view that a teacher's main function is to help others to learn and, above all, to think for themselves. As part of this philosophy, he set great store by Kipling's 'six honest serving men' (What, Why, When, How, Where and Who). He promoted their use through his checklists, which he saw as providing stimuli for yet wider questioning. 'They are,' he said, 'designed to ask some of the questions which are important to effectiveness. They are not exhaustive and there are many more questions which may be asked on individual topics. Nevertheless, if they persuade managers to question their own approach, they will have succeeded.'

The checklists have already won great acclaim. They appeared originally over a period of years in the journal of what was then the Institute of Training and Development. According to the journal's editor, it was their most popular series ever. Two collections were published by Gower as *35 Checklists for Human Resource Development* and *35 Checklists for Human Resource Management* and the material in this new book represents an edited selection made up of those with the widest appeal.

1 Asking questions

Managers spend a large part of their lives at work asking and answering questions, although relatively few are conscious of the various types of questions open to them. Recognizing the different forms that questions can take, and the purposes they serve, may help you to improve your own skill in this respect.

Preliminary diagnosis

1. How often do you ask questions at work? At home? Elsewhere?

2. How many questions, on average, do you estimate you ask each day?

3. To what extent could your performance in asking questions be affecting your job performance? Or relationships at home? Or your reputation in other situations?

4. How many hours' training in asking questions have you undertaken in the past three years? How many books/articles on the subject have you read in the same period? With what result?

5. How do you rate your skill in asking questions sensitively? During conversations at work? During any interviews you conduct? At meetings? On the telephone? At home? Elsewhere?

   - Are you 'above average'? Or merely 'average'? Or even 'below average'?
   - How do you know?
   - How can you know?

1

6. Do you use a wide range of different forms of questions in meeting your various aims? (See Figure 1.1)

   – Are you generally clear about why you are using a particular type of question?
   – What effort do you normally make to 'see' your questions from the other person's point of view?
   – Having asked a question, do you invariably allow the other person thinking time to produce a measured response?
   – How effective are you in encouraging a speaker to continue without saying anything yourself?
   – To what extent do you analyse replies to your questions in terms of:

     • What the person seems to be saying?
     • What can be inferred from what is said and how it is said?
     • What is being conveyed by the whole manner of approach to a reply (the non-verbal signals)?

   – How often in any sort of conversation do you have a tendency to signal the response you want? Or answer your own questions? Or finish speakers' sentences for them? (See Figure 1.2)
   – How far do you avoid asking questions which you think may show your ignorance?
   – How often do you let your mind wander during a conversation and subsequently mishear people's replies to your questions?
   – How often are you asked to repeat your questions?

The future?

7. Do your answers suggest that you could extend your skill in asking questions effectively?

   – What possible action do your answers suggest?
   – What do you believe you should do, if anything? When?

8. What assistance can you seek from colleagues at work? From relatives at home? From others elsewhere? Who will you involve? Who should you involve?

9. Having decided what you will do, and within what time frame, what monitoring is appropriate? How will you measure your progress? When?

Question type	Purpose	Question form	Illustrations
Open	To establish rapport	Contact	Introductory questions/ comments to establish the first superficial relationship and to put respondent at ease, e.g. reference to mutually-shared experiences, unusual leisure interests
	To explore broad background information	General	'Please tell me about ...?'
	To explore opinions/attitudes	Opinion seeking	'How do you feel about ...?' 'What do you think about ...?'
		Trailer	Making a broad comment on a subject and then pausing in anticipation of a response (i.e. the question is hidden)
Probe	To show interest/ encouragement	Non-verbal noises	'Ummm?' 'Er?' 'Ah?' 'Oh?' 'Hmmm?' together with appropriate facial expressions (smiles, raised eyebrows) and head movements
		Supportive statements	'I see ...?' 'And then ...?' 'That's interesting ...?' (i.e. tell me more)
		Key word repetition	Repetition of one or two words to encourage further response
		Mirror	Repetition of short reply as a query
	To seek further information	Simple interrogative	'Why?' 'Why not?'

Figure 1.1 Some question forms

Question type	Purpose	Question form	Illustrations
		The pause	Allied to various non-verbal signals
		Comparative	'How do your responsibilities now compare with those in your last job?'
		Extension	'How do you mean?' 'Can you tell me more about that?'
		Hypothetical	'What would you do if . . .?' 'How would you feel if . . .?'
	To explore in detail particular opinions/attitudes	Opinion investigation	'Why do you feel that way?'
			'Do you have any other reasons for feeling as you do?'
		The reflection	'You think that . . .?' 'It seems to you that . . .?' 'You feel that . . .?'
	To demonstrate understanding/ clarify information already given	Summary	'As I understand it . . .?' 'If I've got it right . . .?' 'So what you're saying is . . .?'
Closed	To establish specific facts/ information	Yes/no response	'Are you . . .?' 'Do you . . .?' 'Have you . . .?'
		Identification of person, time, location, number	'How many people do you have reporting to you?' 'How long did you have that job?'

Figure 1.1   concluded

Question type	Purpose	Question form	Illustrations
Counter-productive	To prompt desired answer	Leading	'I take it you believe that . . .?' 'You don't *really* think that . . . do you?' 'You must admit that . . .?' 'Isn't it a fact that . . .?'
	To confuse or mislead	Marathon	Asking a question in a rambling, incomprehensible way
		Trick	'Do you drink?'
		Multiple	Two or more questions presented as a package. 'You did say you wouldn't mind being away from home occasionally? Oh and you do have a current driving licence, don't you? I presume it's clean? And, er, by the way . . .?' etc.
		Ambiguous	'What about games?'
	To prevent respondent saying anything	Rhetorical	Answering your own questions: 'Do you . . .? Of course you do. I always say that . . .'

Figure 1.2   Question forms to be avoided

2   Assertiveness: First steps

Responding assertively to people and events is one of the requirements for personal success. For most people it is an acquired skill: it can be learned much like any other. To develop your own approach means first taking stock of the ways in which you behave now. The following questions will help you to analyse the beliefs which underpin your behaviour and also provide a springboard for any action you may care to take in becoming more assertive.

1. What sort of person are you? What would be the answers of those who know you?

2. To what extent do you genuinely take responsibility for your own behaviour? For the things you say and do at home, at work and elsewhere? And the ways in which you say them? And do them?

3. Do people have a tendency to hurt or insult you with the things they say about you? And to you?

4. How often do you allow others to make your decisions for you? To manipulate you into making decisions that they want you to make?

5. Just how much do you shift the blame on to others for whatever happens to you?

    – If your answer is 'never', are you sure?
    – Are you ever anxious about the outcome of such events?

6. How satisfied are you with your job currently?

    – Why do you feel this way?
    – What events/people are responsible for your reply?

7. What personal development plans have you initiated and followed through in the last six months? In the six months before that?

8. What do your answers to the previous questions say about you?
   - Do they suggest that you are a comparatively submissive or passive sort of person? One who reacts to events? One who denies responsibility? And who expects and allows others to make his or her decisions?
   - If such descriptions are not typical of your behaviour, what descriptions would be more accurate?

9. How far would it be true to say that rather than allowing others to make decisions for you, the reverse applies? That you have a tendency to make others' decisions for them? ('What you should do is obviously to . . .')

10. Do you ever have to criticize people? To hurt or insult them with the things you say? If so, how often does this happen?

11. What beliefs about life do you hold? Is one of them that you expect people to live their lives by similar (i.e. your) standards?

12. How often do you interrupt when someone is talking? How often do you change the subject to one you wish to discuss? Just how far do you hear, rather than listen?

13. Are you a perfectionist? Do you expect perfection from others? Do you exclude the possibility of people making mistakes?
   - How often do you over-react when mistakes are made?
   - Do you tend to 'nit-pick'?

14. To what extent could it be said that you block people's progress at work? And deny them job satisfaction?

15. What do your answers to questions 9–14 say about you?
   - Do they suggest that you are a rather aggressive sort of person? One who is particularly decisive on behalf of others? One who does not suffer fools gladly? Who lives by high standards and expects others to do likewise?
   - If such descriptions are no more typical of your behaviour than the descriptions included in questions 3–7, what others would be more accurate?

16. Would people say that you have a tendency to manage without hurting them or damaging their self-esteem? That you are a good listener?

17. Do you tend to make the occasional mistake and, having done so, accept responsibility for the consequences?

18. Do you encourage people to make their own decisions? ('What do you think you ought to do?')

19. Can you remain cool in your dealings with people, even when provoked?

20. Do you make your own personal decisions? Are you truly independent? Are you sure? Again, do you encourage others to take a similar stance?

21. Are you the sort of person who genuinely helps others to develop themselves? To gain added job satisfaction?

22. What do your answers to questions 16–21 say about you?

    – Do they suggest that you act within your rights as a person? That you are proactive rather than reactive? That you are a realist?
    – That your temper is under firm control? And that you encourage others to act in a similar way?

23. Do your answers to *all* the previous questions tend to indicate that your behaviour approximates more to one particular category as illustrated in Figure 2.1?

Questions 3–7	Questions 9–14	Questions 16–21
Submissive	Aggressive	Assertive

Figure 2.1 Types of behaviour

24. Whatever your response, is it worth probing in more detail into the beliefs surrounding what might be called your 'typical' behaviour, as illustrated in Figure 2.2?

25. What is your reaction to the descriptions in Figure 2.2? Which set of beliefs seem to describe better the aims of your own behaviour? Are these beliefs a distortion of the likely results as illustrated in Figure 2.3? Or are they an accurate reflection?

Submissive	Aggressive	Assertive
– people will like and accept you, and therefore not hurt you because you are so amenable – you will lead an undemanding, easy life – you won't attract trouble: the chances of getting hurt will be low but you can't be sure – your decisions will be made for you	– you will get things done your way – you will bend people to your will – they will respect, even be afraid of, you – you will hide any weaknesses by attacking them and exposing their own weaknesses – you will inspire confidence and progress in your career	– you will develop and maintain workable relationships with people – you will base these relationships on openness, trust, consistency of treatment, and on being an active listener – you will not accept being a target for manipulation or attack

Figure 2.2   Conscious and subconscious beliefs associated with each type of behaviour

Submission	Aggression	Assertion
– you will be despised by many as lacking courage, not knowing your own mind, vacillating, weak and many more negative epithets – people will be continually frustrated in their dealings with you and will show it – you will not take control of your own destiny and your life will be drab, unexciting and friendless – you will lack personal integrity and self-esteem and your physical and mental health will suffer	– you will inspire antagonism, dislike, even fear in many people – you will attract extensive opposition from sturdier souls – your efforts will be nullified, even sabotaged, where the opportunity arises – people will not trust you – your stress level will be high – you will have an unrealistic view of your own integrity, and worse, you will be blissfully unaware of and reject any indications of the real situation – you stand a chance of being physically assaulted	– you will manage potentially stressful situations effectively – you will extend your self-confidence and inspire confidence in others – you will avoid manipulation by others and deflect attack – you will have a realistic view of your own integrity and will make every effort to keep it intact – you will maintain and exude a sense of well-being

Figure 2.3   Likely results of the behaviour

26. Having reflected on your responses to this checklist, what action could you take to develop yourself? Are there elements of submissive or aggressive behaviour which you want to eliminate?

27. What specifically should you do? And on further reflection, what will you do? Over what time-scale? How will you monitor your progress? And who else could be involved? Who should be involved?

28. Will you record your commitment to development? And genuinely assess your progress? How often?

29. If you are not prepared to do anything having answered the previous questions, what are you saying about yourself? Do you believe the answer? Are you truly happy with it?

3 Assertiveness: Strengthening the skills

Having taken the action you considered necessary to become more assertive (see Checklist 2) it may be helpful to check periodically whether you are maintaining progress. Such analyses will help you to strengthen your existing skills and provide a basis for any further action you consider appropriate. The following questions are designed to help you start the process.

1. What action, if any, have you taken as a result of reading Checklist 2?

2. To what extent do you find yourself still being either submissive or aggressive in particular social situations? Have you behaved in the following ways at any time in the past month and, if so, how often?

    a. Standing up for yourself without upsetting people
    b. Losing your temper with people
    c. Admitting when you don't know the answer to a question
    d. Feeling embarrassed when somebody compliments you
    e. Feeling you have been made to look a little foolish by what someone says to you
    f. Declining what you believe to be unreasonable demands or requests made of you, without upsetting people
    g. Prompting others to make decisions for you
    h. Fighting back when you are criticized
    i. Insisting on your rights as a customer or employee without being discourteous or offensive
    j. Feeling you have to put people in their place
    k. Offering advice on what people ought to do in particular situations
    l. Feeling your self-respect threatened by what some people say to you
    m. Saying self-critical things to people (e.g. 'I'm just no good at that', 'I'm useless at drawing', 'I'm hopeless with figures')
    n. Feeling resentful at the way some people treat you

    o. Being proud that you are one of life's competitors
    p. Apologizing for what you have said or done
    q. Finding that people become irritated with you
    r. Finding that you have to criticize people for what they say
    s. Interrupting people as they are speaking
    t. Feeling that you are in control of your life

Note: You probably know your IQ. You could begin to assess your AQ (Assertiveness Quotient) by scoring your responses to the 20 questions above. For questions a, c, f, l and t, score 5 each time you answered 'almost always', 4 for 'often', 3 for 'sometimes', 2 for 'rarely' and 1 for 'almost never'. For all remaining questions reverse your scores (5 for 'almost never', 4 for 'rarely', 3 for 'sometimes', 2 for 'often', and 1 for 'almost always').

3. What do your answers suggest about the ways in which you have actually behaved in the past month? Do you want to become more assertive? In which particular ways?

    – Dealing with criticism of what you do?
    – Dealing with criticism of what you are?
    – Initiating and accepting discussions of both your strengths and limitations?
    – Actively prompting criticism?
    – Becoming a better listener?
    – Recognizing the signals in conversation which indicate what is concerning the speaker?
    – Making your point of view heard without becoming stressed?

4. Would it help to consider whether you could develop your approach to dealing more effectively with these (potentially stressful) situations? How often do you use the type of response shown in Figure 3.1?

5. Having reflected on the responses illustrated in Figure 3.1, do you respond similarly without apologizing? Do you, can you, accept appropriate criticism, absorb sarcasm and verbal bullying *without becoming defensive?* Or aggressive?

6. If you can develop this approach to dealing with potentially stressful situations do you recognize that by doing so you are giving yourself every chance to control your life positively, to be your own person?

7. So what are you proposing to do now? Over the next week? The next month? A longer period?

Situation	Response
Criticism of your actions	'Yes, perhaps you're right' 'Yes, it does look as if I might have made a mistake there' 'No, perhaps I shouldn't have done that'
Criticism of your personality	'That's true, I can upset some people' 'Yes, I accept that I am insensitive on occasions'
Prompting discussion which extends your self-knowledge	'I am rather concerned about what will happen when . . .' 'In that meeting, I felt that . . .' 'I don't know the answer to that one'
Prompting criticism	'What is it particularly about me that upsets you?' 'Is there anything else you would like to say about me?'
Becoming a better listener	'From what you were saying just now . . .' 'You feel that . . .' 'It seems to you that . . .'
Making your voice heard whilst remaining cool	'I understand what you're saying, but I feel that . . .' 'I appreciate that, but I still feel that . . .' 'Yes, I appreciate your difficulties, but I still feel that . . .'

Figure 3.1 Framing your responses

4 Assessing staff performance

Most organizations require managers to review the job performance of their staff periodically. But for this to be a useful exercise it must be done objectively. There are a number of pitfalls to beware of, and this checklist provides a useful aid, with guidelines on how they might be avoided.

1. To what extent are you required, as part of your job, to assess the work performance of your own staff?

    - At the end of a probationary period?
    - As part of a periodical (annual?) appraisal process?
    - As part of a disciplinary process?
    - At the conclusion of a training/development programme?
    - For some other reason?

        • If so, why?

2. How far do you feel competent in judging people's performance objectively?

    - What evidence have you which supports any claim to objectivity in judging the performance of others?
    - What evidence is there which relates any claim to objectivity?

3. Could the basis of your judgement of others be developed? To what extent? Do you want to improve?

4. Figure 4.1 illustrates a range of errors in judgements which are worth considering in detail. How many of these errors may be present in your own judgement?

Error (The effect)	Description	Definitely absent from my judgement processes	Possibly present in my judgement processes	Definitely present in my judgement processes
Halo	Appraising someone high in all aspects of the job because of one outstanding characteristic.			
Horns	Appraising someone low in all aspects of the job because of one outstanding bad characteristic.			
Logical error	Appraising similarly those factors which appear to be logically related.			
Proximity	Appraising similarly those items adjacent to each other on the appraisal form.			
Surface	Appraising only the more obvious and describable elements of performance at the expense of the less easily definable, but nevertheless important ones.			
Leniency	Appraising individuals more highly than they deserve. Appraisers who are aware of this possibility tend to overcompensate for it and rate lower than they should.			
Central tendency	Avoiding the high and low extremes on a rating scale and concentrating scores in the middle.			
Contrast	Using personal standards as the reference point. The individual is then judged in contrast (opposite) to these standards.			
Similar-to-me	Appraising more favourably if the individual is perceived as being similar to the appraiser.			
Overall	Prejudging overall improvement or deterioration in performance. Subsequently the ratings of individual factors are adjusted to comply with this prejudged overall result – usually to show an improvement.			
Recency	Being over-influenced by recent events, either favourably or unfavourably.			

Figure 4.1 Errors and beliefs about the judgement process

Error (The effect)	Description	Definitely absent from my judgement processes	Possibly present in my judgement processes	Definitely present in my judgement processes
Differential accuracy	Appraising less accurately when the behaviour being evaluated is unfavourable rather than favourable.			
Spillover	Allowing past appraisals to influence the current appraisal.			
Blind-spot	Failing to recognize certain types of defect because they are the appraiser's own defects.			
Negative	Avoiding negative appraisal because of perceived likely difficulties in the interview subsequently. Alternatively, using the appraisal as a means of influencing relationships with individuals.			
Naivety	Accepting other people's opinions about the individual under review without due consideration.			
Coincidence	Being over-influenced by easily observable events, for instance a 'lucky break'.			

Figure 4.1   concluded

5. Having reflected on the errors illustrated in Figure 4.1, which ones appear to be the most important for you? Which are less important?

6. Would it be worth discussing your perceptions:
    -   With close colleagues?
        •   Are you a partner in a co-counselling arrangement?
    -   With others?
        •   For example your spouse/partner?

7. Are you now in a position to describe the priorities for action?
    -   What is it that you have decided to do?
    -   Who else is (or should be) involved?
    -   And how will you monitor your own progress in judging people's performance more effectively?

8. If you are proposing to do nothing as a result of reviewing the possible errors, what are you saying about yourself?

- Are you absolutely sure that there is nothing you could do?
- Or should do?
- Are you genuinely happy with your answers?

5 Coaching

The ability and willingness to give guidance and help to staff is an integral part of every manager's role: ability to assess accurately what coaching is appropriate, and willingness to commit time and effort to its achievement. It is this latter factor – willingness – which demands particular self-discipline. It is all too easy to allow good intentions to be buried under other, seemingly more pressing, tasks.

1. If you are a successful manager, what have been the significant factors in your success? Was one factor the positive help (guidance, coaching, counselling) you received from senior managers?

    – Are you still receiving, or would you benefit from, further help now?
    – What does this answer indicate?

2. How seriously do managers in your organization take their responsibilities for developing staff?

    – Are they really aware of the implications of this responsibility?
    – How do you know?

3. Are they devoting as much time as they should to developing the performance of their staff? Are you?

    – To what extent is 'coaching' regarded as an integral part of every management job?
    – Do all managers help to develop the performance of their staff by:

      • Systematically giving them planned tasks to increase their abilities and experience?
      • Evaluating their performance in relation to these planned tasks?
      • Giving appropriate personal guidance to sustain/develop progress towards the target?

- Generally monitoring performance against the time-scale set?

  − If not, what action is indicated?

4. Has a check ever been made in the organization to establish just how much training individual managers have received in coaching techniques?

   − How many individuals have attended practical training sessions outside the organization on the subject? Have any been conducted inside the organization?

     - How many work days were involved last year? How many so far this year? Spread over how many managers?

   − Is that really enough when the critical importance of every individual's contribution to success is considered?

5. If the (further) commitment of managers to the advantages of coaching is to be secured, has the practical application of the technique in your organization been fully explored?

   − If so, by whom? With what results?
   − If not, who should be responsible for doing so?

6. Have the following question areas been explored?

Strategy

7. What are the main areas within individual departments which could provide opportunities for coaching?

   The work itself
   − What are the main problems currently? Potentially?
   − Which can be used to provide a practical learning situation for staff?
   − Have the opportunities for coaching been identified?
   − Can targets (end states) be derived from these opportunities and closely specified?

   Individual staff
   − What shortcomings in attitudes, skills and/or knowledge have been identified, and need to be overcome?
   − Can targets for improvement/development be specified?

8. Can coaching priorities be set, based on the above?

Tactics

9. Considering the priorities in order, what action is appropriate to meet individual learning needs in terms of:

   – The situation itself?

     • What preparation is necessary?
     • Will the relevance and value of the assignment be made absolutely clear? How?

   – The personality/skills of the manager concerned?

     • Interpersonal skills?
     • Listening skills?

   – The personality of the individual concerned?

     • Existing skills and knowledge?
     • General capability?

10. What timing and specific coaching approach do these answers suggest?

    – What will be delegated? How? When?
    – Will the appropriate authority to act be granted?

Control

11. How will progress towards the targets be measured? What yardsticks are appropriate? What feedback is necessary?

    – Will the control be flexible and amenable to modification?
    – How will each individual's thinking be stimulated? Can the control be by watchful neglect?
    – Could such an approach help to build a sense of trust?
    – Will each individual be given every chance to monitor his or her own progress?

Further action

12. If managers are committed to this approach, would it be worthwhile evaluating individual managers' use of coaching by periodically asking them the following questions? And asking these questions of yourself?

    – What plans have you for coaching each one of your staff in the next six months?

- What lessons have you learned from recent coaching situations? Are you applying them now?

  • Has your own management style developed?

- What benefits has coaching produced in your department?

  • How does individual performance now compare with what it was six months ago? Twelve months ago?

- If it has not improved markedly, are you spending enough of your time on coaching?
- Do you truly believe that by helping your own staff to grow you are growing yourself? If not, what does this answer indicate about your own managerial prospects (see question 1)?

6 Corporate culture

The tone of an organization – illustrated by the ways things are done, how people behave, the ceremonies and rituals – plays a vital role in shaping people's expectations. Understanding the nature of your own organization's culture, and its impact on day-to-day operations, is an important ingredient in the decisions you take.

Background analysis

1. What does 'corporate culture' mean in your organization?

    -   To you?
    -   To top management?
    -   To supervisors and managers at different levels?
    -   To everyone else?

2. To what extent do these views differ? How do you know?

    -   Has a check ever been made?
    -   If so, when was it last made?
    -   Is a further check necessary now?

3. Could anyone in your organization have made the following comments?

    -   'Corporate culture? What's that?'
    -   'There's no such thing.'
    -   'This company is heading for trouble. The culture is wrong.'
    -   'Attitudes in this place are fossilized.'
    -   'Don't ask me, I only work here.'
    -   'We don't need "culture". We know what we've got to do.'

- 'Our culture is simply that management is scared stiff of him upstairs.'
- 'Talk about culture . . . There's only one person who makes decisions in this place.'
- 'Culture is important, but what can we do about it?'

4. How important is it for the decision-takers on your organization to be absolutely clear about the impact of 'culture' on your organization?

    - Can you identify the 'shared meanings' in your organization? The accepted values? The beliefs about what is important? The sayings people use? The ways in which things are done?

5. How critical are these 'shared meanings' to the way you do your job? To the ways others do their jobs?

    - Are people agreed on why the organization exists?
    - How far do people at different levels agree what is of fundamental importance to your organization?

6. Whatever your answers, what is being done to ensure that the organization's culture is appropriate to today's environment? And to tomorrow's?

Diagnosing the prevailing culture

7. What does your organization stand for?

    - What are its objectives? Growth? Profit? Customer satisfaction? Market share? Product development? Service excellence? Survival? Or what?
    - What is the view of top management?
    - What are the views of managers at different levels?
    - What are the views of everyone else?

    Do these views fit with the culture the organization is trying to foster?

8. What seems to be the top priority for the 'foot soldiers' in your organization?

    - Staying out of the firing line?
    - Doing a good job?
    - Pushing for more money or promotion?
    - Keeping their jobs?

    What is the organization's view on these issues? How has it been made known?

9. What are the general expectations within the organization in terms of:

    - Behaviour?
    - Dress?
    - Timekeeping?
    - Acceptance of authority?
    - Work performance?

    What other 'marks of acceptance' are there? What does this tell you about the 'tone' of the organization?

10. What are regarded as personal virtues by the organization? Achievement? Survival? Integrity? Loyalty? Honesty? Self-sacrifice? Being behind a desk? Hard work? Commitment? Or what?

    - Again, what does your answer tell you about the 'tone' of the organization?

11. What special language is used?

    - What initials or other jargon is used?
    - What technical language is used?
    - What is the official motto?
    - What is the unofficial motto?

    Why do members of the organization use this special language?

12. What are the organization's rituals and ceremonies? Parties? Outings? Long-service presentations? Other events? Ways of doing things? What do they tell you about the way in which the organization sees itself?

13. How do people feel that they are regarded by the organization?

    - Do they regard themselves as exchanging their labour for pay?
    - Do they feel part of a family?
    - Do they feel part of a community?
    - Do they see themselves merely as sellers in a market-place? If not, how do they see themselves?

14. What status distinctions are there? Separate dining rooms? Special parking spaces? Other privileges? Access to secretarial and other resources?

    - How do people feel about them?

15. Does the organization have heroes?

    - Why are they regarded as heroic?
    - What does this tell you about the culture?

16. How positive have your answers been to these questions?

    – What does the strength of your response indicate about your organization's culture?
    – What would prevent a newcomer from being accepted?
    – What would result in an existing employee being 'cold shouldered'?
    – How strongly are beliefs and values held?

17. Do these beliefs and values apply across the entire organization?

    – Do they apply across particular divisions/departments?

    Or are they peculiar to specific work groups?

Cultural 'fit'

18. Does the prevailing culture enhance your organization's performance?

    – How particularly does it help?
    – Does it help corporate goals to be achieved?
    – Does it make communication easier?
    – Does it encourage greater co-operation?
    – Are staff motivated to perform more effectively? How?

19. Or does the culture hinder performance?

    – How prevalent is 'group think'?
    – Is there any noticeable entrenched resistance to change? Or to announcing bad news?

    In what other ways might the culture detract from corporate goals?

20. What steps are being taken now to ensure that the values of prospective entrants fit the organizational culture?

    – What values, attitudes or beliefs would exclude a candidate during the selection process?
    – How are key values conveyed to the candidate?

21. To what extent do new entrants suffer from 'culture shock'?

    – Is this contributing to an induction crisis?
    – What action, if any, does your answer suggest?

22. How are new entrants inducted into the culture?

    – Through a formal programme?
    – Through a staff handbook?

- Informally by talking to 'old hands'?
- Picking it up as they go along?

Is a system of 'mentoring' in place? If so, how were the mentors chosen? What criteria were used?

23. In your organization, how are cultural values communicated? Through memos? Through the company newspaper? Employee reports? Meetings? Rewards (e.g. promotion, recognition)? Punishments (e.g. being passed over, demoted)? By the actions of management?

    - Or how?
    - In what other significant ways are these values communicated?

24. What is the attitude within the organization towards 'mavericks' who publicly behave contrary to cultural expectations?

    - Are they ignored? Are they isolated? Are they encouraged? Are they tolerated?
    - How precisely are they treated?

Cultural development

25. Is there a need for cultural change?

    - How much is company policy resisted?
    - In what particular ways is it resisted?
    - Is there a ready explanation for such attitudes?
    - How do people feel about the introduction of new technology?
    - To what extent is the current level of productivity acceptable?

    In general terms, would you say that morale is high? Or does it need to be improved?

26. How well do people cope with any changes now? Do they fear change? Or do they welcome it? Do they accept it as inevitable? What does your answer say about the way the organization operates?

27. How are the advantages of changes put to people?

    - Are the likely repercussions of any changes reviewed before the event? Are you sure? How do you know?
    - What more could be done in the future to ensure that such reviews are more effective?
    - Who should be involved? Are they?

28. How could such change be introduced?

- By example? Whose example would be particularly appropriate?
- By coercion? Have the implications of such an approach been thought through fully?
- By reward? What methods specifically would achieve the desired result?
- By persuasion?
- By participation/involvement?

29. During discussions on strategic change is the prevailing culture within the organization considered fully? Are the cultural implications of tactical decisions also considered in detail?

   - Is the culture appropriate for involving people fully in deciding the particular parameters of any changes?
   - What would happen if people did not co-operate, particularly as a result of poor communication?
   - What are the wider implications of your answers to these questions?

30. How much influence do you personally have in shaping the way in which your organization operates?

   - What action does your answer suggest?

31. How does this review of the way your organization operates affect your own role?

32. What action on your part is appropriate? How soon should such action be taken? Within what time-frame?

7 Creative problem solving

The western world has tended to emphasize an analytical, systematic approach to problem solving. It certainly offers one useful route, but there are other, more creative, methods. Organizations are building up their repertoires of these to enable them to bring the whole range of techniques to bear upon problems. Reviewing your habitual approach to problem solving can open the door to increasing the number of techniques at your disposal.

1. How far do you tend to rely on an analytical, systematic approach to the problems you encounter?

2. Reflecting on the problems you have encountered in the past month, how many did you subject to such a systematic analysis before deciding what should be done?

3. And how many were tackled in a non-systematic, lateral thinking, creative way? Transfer your responses to Figure 7.1.

Analytical responses	Creative responses	A combination of analytical and creative responses
Number of problems solved this way	Number of problems solved this way	Number of problems solved this way

Figure 7.1 Your preferred responses to problem solving: past month

4. Now review the numbers you have written in. Is there a balance (roughly equal numbers in each sector)? Or is there a significantly higher number in one sector? If so, which?

5. To what extent do your responses indicate that you prefer to think analytically? That you like to take a systematic, logical, step-by-step approach to solving problems and making decisions? Or do your responses suggest that you adopt a much more intuitive, imaginative stance? Or a combination of the two?

6. Which quadrant illustrated in Figure 7.2 do you believe represents most accurately your preferred thinking style?

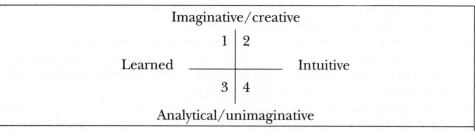

Key to quadrant sectors

1. Techniques of imaginative and creative thinking include brain-storming, morphological analysis, random stimulation, attribute listing, forced relationships, checklists, reverse brainstorming and mind mapping. These techniques can be learned (see Figure 7.5).

2. Interactive solutions to problems ('flashes of inspiration') – the 'Eureka' insight – is relatively rare for most people.

1 and 2 represent divergent thinking, thought by some to originate in the right brain.

3. This quadrant represents the systematic, logical response to problems: an analytical approach which is learned. Efficient use leads to predictable solutions.

4. An analytical and unimaginative thinking style which may look intuitive because steps in the logical thinking are 'hurdled' (missed out) and solutions appear impracticable. They are not.

3 and 4 represent convergent thinking and are thought by some to originate in the left brain.

Figure 7.2   Matrix of thinking styles

    – What are the implications of your response for your own longer-term development?

    – Would it be worth extending your skill at producing creative responses to problem situations?

    – Or do you believe your capability in this respect is limited at an absolute low? If so, why?

- **Thinking convergently**
  We have a tendency to break problems down into their constituent elements and draw conclusions from their inter-relationship. Some would say that any conclusion is an 'end-state' that blocks further thinking. Few are willing to think divergently.
- **The desire to find the 'one right answer'**
  Experience suggests that there are 'righter' answers and 'wronger' answers but very rarely one right answer. The great majority of problems are amenable to an even larger number of possible solutions.
- **The desire to conform**
  Few people are willing to avoid conforming to some assumed norm. Such behaviour is considered to be eccentric – somehow it is abnormal. Closely allied are the following blockages.
- **The fear of looking foolish**
  Nobody actively wants to look foolish. To step outside the social conventions of what is considered acceptable behaviour is to invite a charge of being 'stupid' or 'foolish'.
- **Evaluating ideas too quickly**
  Everyone likes to order their own personal world, and such order is founded on past experience. Personal experience is nevertheless a two-edged sword: experience can be both positive and negative, and we may be living in the past without realizing it. People tend to jump to conclusions. Figure 7.4 illustrates some of the ways in which we evaluate suggestions based on our own past experience, and such experience may be blocking our thinking.
- **Not challenging the obvious**
  We all have a tendency to accept what we see as 'facts' without question. Again social conventions dictate that we do things in particular ways, although the ways themselves may have been decided many generations ago. 'Why'? and 'What if . . .'? questions are important weapons in the armoury of the non-conventional thinker. Are you an example of 'programming' not to ask awkward questions? How often do you challenge assumptions?

Figure 7.3 Creative thinking: some self-imposed blockages

7. Even if you believe that the potential for creative and imaginative thinking is missing from your make-up, might it be worth examining the background to this belief? How many of the possible blockages to creative thinking illustrated in Figure 7.3 seem to apply to you?

8. What do your responses to Figure 7.4 tell you about yourself? To what extent are you happy with your answers? Would you prefer to develop your competence at thinking more creatively? At eliminating the self-imposed blockage(s) which apply particularly to you?

- 'It would be all right in theory, but not in practice.'
  There is nothing so practical as a good theory.
- 'Staff will never accept it.'
  How do you know without consulting them?
- 'That's been tried before.'
  People and situations change. Is the situation comparable? Are the people?
- 'That hasn't been tried before.'
  So what? Is that a sufficient reason?
- 'It couldn't be done.'
  Why not? How do you know?
- 'The time can't be spared.'
  Is this a sufficient reason? Can't time be made if necessary?
- 'It would mean more work.'
  Of course! Although it may result in more effective use of your time in the future and an improved reputation for getting things done!

Figure 7.4   Evaluating ideas: jumping to conclusions

9. If so, consider the techniques listed in Figure 7.5.

   – Which of the techniques are particularly useful weapons in your personal armoury of skills now? Which others could be useful if you are prepared to incorporate them within your thinking processes?
   – Which techniques could be useful for the staff for whom you are responsible personally? For others in your organization?
   – What action on your part is indicated? How soon should such action be taken? After consultation with whom?

10. Is sufficient effort devoted now to developing creative thinking in your organization? In this context how do you define the word 'sufficient'? What do your answers suggest could be done? What should be done? By whom? When?

Technique		Used now	Not used now	Could prove useful
(Serial) Brainstorming	Generating as many ideas as possible in a group within a specified time-frame. The ideas are evaluated subsequently.			
(Reverse) Brainstorming (The 'devil's advocate')	Generating as many reasons as possible in a group within a specified time-scale as to why an idea may fail.			
Morphological analysis	Where the variables within a situation are recombined in new ways.			
Random stimulation	Using a reference book (dictionary, encyclopaedia) to choose a word at random. Subsequently reviewing the application of this word to the problem.			
Attribute listing	Generating a list of the major attributes of an idea to further stimulate generation of ideas.			
Forced relationships	Taking seemingly unrelated ideas and questioning what new idea would be produced by combining them.			
Checklists	Using a list of questions.			
Mind-mapping to generate new ideas.*	Tony Buzan's idea for recording and further generating ideas, mind-mapping is an application of multi-coloured spider diagrams.			

* Tony Buzan, *Use Your Head*, revised and extended edition 1982, The British Broadcasting Corporation, London.

Figure 7.5   Some techniques for enhancing imaginative thinking

8 Delegation

Managers who do not delegate tasks will fail themselves, their staff, and the organization they represent. Attempting everything personally, they feel harassed and overworked despite ever-increasing effort.

To break this vicious circle requires self-discipline: it can often seem easier to do jobs which may take longer to explain than complete. The discipline lies in overcoming this selfishness to consider the needs of staff who want to grow. Unless the right tasks are delegated to the right people at the right time, they will not grow – and neither will you.

Preliminary diagnosis

1. To what extent do you plan your job? Does it have any tendency to plan you?

2. How effectively do you manage your time? Whatever your response, are you sure you know?

3. Do you take work home regularly?

4. Do you work much longer hours than your staff?

5. Do you have difficulties in meeting deadlines?

6. Do you spend too much time on detail?

7. Do people come to you too often for instructions on:
   - What should be done?
   - When it should be done?

- How it should be done?
- Who should do it?
- Where it should be done?
- Why it should be done?

8. Where is your personal stress threshold now? In front of you? Behind you? In either case, how far away is it?

9. What are the strengths, weaknesses, opportunities and threats presented by your current workload?

   - Take a critical 'snapshot' now: to what extent are you achieving your main accountabilities? What are your strong points? What are the flaws in your personal productivity? Currently? Potentially? How could your answers be used to consolidate your position? Or be used against you?

10. What action is suggested by your answers to these questions? To what extent could a more effective distribution of work ease the burden?

11. Could your present approach to delegating tasks be modified or extended? Should it be? Just how far would you like to improve?

Preparing to delegate

12. Which parts of your work could, and should, be delegated? Have you thought through the possibilities? In detail?. What tasks can you identify?

13. In the context of your section/department activities, how important is each one?

14. Who should do what? Can you match the task to the person? The person to the task?

The task

- What are the priorities within the task?
- Within what time-frame must the task be completed?
- What are the cost limits?
- What resources can be called on?
- What additional information will be needed?
- What potential problems might arise? Who should deal with them?
- What decisions must be referred back?
- What contingency planning is necessary?

The person

- Does the task require a particular level of existing skills, knowledge or attitudes?
- Is the task being used to provide a valuable learning experience?
- Who could, and would, benefit most from involvement/responsibility?
- How does the task fit into the person's current workload?
- Are you clear about why you are delegating to the person concerned?
- Is the degree of risk acceptable?

Taking action

15. What approach is most appropriate?

Location

- Where should the task be delegated?

  - Where others can hear?
  - Where others should hear?
  - In private?

Timing

- When should the task be delegated?

  - What would be the best moment?

Method

- How should the task be delegated?

  - Verbally?
  - Or in writing?
  - If verbally, is a request or an instruction most appropriate?

Focus of briefing

- Will the briefing concentrate on the critical parameters of the task? And on personal accountability for results?
- What degree of independent planning by the person will be appropriate?
- How much flexibility should be built into the task?
- Is 'watchful neglect' appropriate? Or should the control be tighter?
- Will you delegate the right to be wrong?
- Will necessary monitoring arrangements be agreed? And followed subsequently?

 – Will a date/time be fixed for the debriefing/feedback session?

Communication net

 – Who needs to know what you have delegated and to whom? Whom might it also be useful to inform?

Follow-up

16. What was the effect of your delegation?

On the person concerned

 – How well was the task performed?
 – What future coaching/counselling needs can be identified?
 – What was the reaction to your feedback?
 – What action does your answer suggest?

On other staff

 – What have been their reactions?

On yourself

 – In broad terms did your preparation produce the results you wanted?
 – Did you match the task to the person effectively?
 – Did you save time? Did you use the saving productively?
 – What action on your part do your answers suggest?

17. What have you learned which will be helpful in delegating tasks in the future? How will you make sure that the learning is not forgotten for the next time?

9 Disciplinary interviewing

At some time in a manager's career, almost inevitably, a situation arises which requires a disciplinary interview. For this to be of benefit to the individual(s) involved and to the organization, careful preparation is essential. You need to have all the facts available, plus a plan of the interview – and a clear idea of the objectives you wish to achieve.

Objectives

1. Do you accept that there are two primary objectives in taking any disciplinary action:

    - To punish?
    - To deter people from committing similar offences?

Preparation

2. Are you aware of any strong feelings that you may have for or against the person to be disciplined?

3. Have you allowed sufficient time for:

    - Preparation?
    - The interview itself?

4. Have you considered the following questions during your preparation:

    - What is the offence?
    - Why did it occur?

  - Will disciplinary action be the most effective way of dealing with the matter?
  - Following the organization's disciplinary procedure, who should be present at the interview?
  - What other relevant background information is there?

The interview

5. Will you make sure that you:

  - Adopt a calm and methodical approach?
  - Ask the individual to give his/her story?
  - Elicit the facts and the individual's agreement to them?
  - Repeat the key points to confirm your own understanding?
  - Look for the reasons why the individual acted as he/she did?
  - State clearly and firmly the disciplinary action you propose to take?

6. Will you also make sure that you do *not*:

  - Become drawn into a personal argument?
  - Lose your self-control?
  - Threaten?
  - 'Flannel'?
  - Demoralize or humiliate?

After the interview

7. - Did the interview achieve your objectives?
  - Was your handling of the matter constructive and positive?
  - Did the individual accept that he/she had done wrong?
  - Did he/she appreciate the implications of his/her error?
  - Has the same error been prevented from recurring?
  - Was justice not only done, but seen to be done?
  - Have you complied with your organization's written disciplinary procedure?
  - Have details of the disciplinary action taken been recorded for future reference?

10 External training courses

Even the best run organizations sometimes need to use external training courses. Alternative ways of meeting the need should be considered first, however, and if an external course seems most appropriate then every effort should be made to ensure a maximum return on the costs involved.

1. Have the training needs of the individual(s) concerned been identified? Precisely? For instance, if a supposed communications training need has been identified, what particular type of communication is involved? Oral? Or written? If written, is the need to improve performance in writing memos, reports, business letters or what?

2. How was the need identified? Was it done by consultation? With the individual(s) concerned? By whom? If it was not immediate supervision, why?

3. Is the need for:

   – Initial training?
   – Booster training?
   – Retraining?

4. Having pinpointed the training need, have you also identified the standard of performance required as a result of the training? With those concerned? Have the criteria of success been established? Have these criteria been quantified where possible?

5. Once the parameters have been established, have you examined thoroughly all alternative methods of meeting the need? On a cost-effectiveness basis?

6. If, as a result, using an external training course appears to be the most effective means, have you considered the following points?

    – How many staff need training?
    – For how long?
    – When should they be trained?
    – What are the priorities?
    – How should they be trained?
    – Where should they be trained?
    – At what cost?

7. Have you considered, on a cost-effectiveness basis, the possibility of mounting an in-company course with the help of outside speakers to fill the training need?

8. What would be the other advantages of this approach (e.g. a tailor-made course concentrating on your organization's policies/practices/needs)?

9. If this approach is not appropriate, how do you choose the most suitable external course?

10. Does your organization maintain a 'register' of courses on offer at different levels and for different occupational groups?

11. Who is (or should be) responsible for its regular updating?

12. Are you aware of the various bodies which provide information on course availability (e.g. your local TEC or LEC, regional management centre, the various professional institutes, research associations, etc.)? Is your organization on their mailing lists? If not, what action should be taken? By whom?

13. How is the effectiveness of particular external courses checked? If assessment does not take place prior to use, why not?

14. When a particular course has been chosen, is the individual concerned briefed fully before attending the course? Is agreement reached with him or her on:

    – Why attendance is necessary?
    – What is expected in terms of pre-course preparation?
    – What is expected during the course? And on return from the course?

15. When the individual returns from an external course is he or she asked to prepare a critical report on the course against the criteria of success

established at the outset? If not, why not? If so, who is responsible for reviewing the feedback and following up with any necessary action? Is it done? By the right person?

16. During the last financial year, how many employee days were devoted to external training? How does this figure compare with that for training carried out within the organization? What were the total costs of each type of training? How does each figure, and the total, compare with the organization's sales turnover in the same period? Was it too much? Or too little? Against what criteria?

17. Is your organization securing its money's worth from using external courses?

11   Handling a grievance

How grievances are handled affects the atmosphere – and productivity – of the workplace. Good employee relations practice will always ensure that grievances are dealt with swiftly and effectively, to prevent molehills becoming mountains. Many organizations have a written grievances procedure, but the key question is whether this is being followed – in the spirit as well as the letter.

1. Do you accept that creating and maintaining the right atmosphere is critical to your success in handling the grievances of your staff?

    – Are you consistent in your attitude?
    – Do you show that you are concerned to right obvious wrongs?
    – When problems arise do you tackle them with determination until a conclusion is reached?
    – Do you keep everyone informed of changes which will affect them?

2. When grievances do arise, have you considered the importance of:

    – Holding the meeting in private?
    – Allowing the person concerned to tell their story without interruptions?
    – Keeping cool?
    – Making notes?
    – Ensuring your own full understanding of the situation?
    – Thinking before you answer?

        • Are other people involved?
        • Are there any precedents?

    – Being aware of your own prejudices and controlling them?

3. Have you also considered the adverse consequences of:

- Delaying tackling the situation?
- Relying on your memory?
- Allowing the discussion to become personal?
- Being drawn into a shouting match?
- Assuming too much?
- Jumping to conclusions?
- Forgetting to record your decision for future reference?

4. Do you accept that the best way of handling a grievance is to deal with it quickly, firmly and consistently?

5. Are you aware that the law requires an employer to specify in an employee's written statement of terms and conditions of employment to whom the employee can take a grievance relating to employment?

6. Are you aware that the Industrial Relations Code of Practice lays down certain recommendations for the handling of grievances? That although these do not have the force of law, they are taken into account in deciding cases by industrial tribunals?

7. Are you aware that these recommendations include the following:
    - That all employees have a right to seek redress for grievances relating to their employment?
    - That each employee must be told how he/she can do so?
    - That grievances should be settled fairly and promptly, and as near as possible to the point of origin?
    - That the procedure should provide, first, for discussion of the grievance between the employee and his immediate superior?
    - That the employee should be accompanied at the next stage of the discussion with management by his employee representative or a work colleague if he so wishes?

8. Can you distinguish between individual and collective grievances?

9. Does your organization have a written grievance procedure which complies with these recommendations?

10. If so, do you have a copy? Do your staff?

11. What is the role of line managers within the procedure?

12. What are the training needs and implications if grievances are to be handled successfully?

12 Interviewing

Your skill at interviewing people has a direct impact on both your professional reputation and the reputation of the organization you represent. Every successful interview, whether it is concerned with selection, discipline, appraisal, termination or more general fact-finding, is underpinned by effective preparation. Planning of both what you want to achieve and how it can be achieved is vital.

Introduction

1. What proportion, in percentage terms, of your job is spent interviewing for any purpose?

    – How much of your working life is devoted to:

       • Choosing people for jobs? (Selection)
       • Discussing task-related issues? (Job performance)
       • Dealing with their grievances? (Grievance)
       • Discussing their job performance with them? (Appraisal)
       • Handling issues of personal conduct at work? (Discipline)
       • Helping them to clarify their problems and make their own decisions? (Counselling)
       • Establishing why they have resigned? (Exit/termination)
       • Any other 'conversations with a purpose'?

2. How important is being able to interview effectively to you *personally*? To what extent does your professional reputation hinge on your skill as an interviewer?

    – What possible action does your answer indicate?

3. How much time do you spend on preparing for particular interviews? Is it enough in your view?

4. How many articles/books on interviewing have you read in the past twelve months?

   – What effect has this reading had on your interviewing performance?

5. How much training in interviewing skills have you undergone in the past five years? Would any booster training be useful now?

6. How often do you discuss your interviewing performance with colleagues? Is that often enough?

   – How often do you invite a colleague to sit in with you on a particular interview (for instance, during selection) to review your performance? When was the last time you filled this role for someone else?

7. How much has your interviewing style changed in the last five years?

   – How has it changed?

8. To what extent do you feel your personal values affect your interviewing style? How far should they?

9. If you were to pinpoint one particular personal skill as being crucial to effective interviewing, what would it be?

   – What other personal skills are appropriate for interviewing purposes?
   – To what extent do you believe you possess these personal skills?
   – What action do your answers to these questions indicate?

10. How far do you consider yourself to be a good judge of people?

   – In what ways do you believe you could improve your judgement of people?

11. To what extent does the law affect your interviewing style and the questions you ask?

   – If you are not absolutely sure, what action is indicated?

12. How important is it, in your view, to follow up the interview decisions you make?

   – To what extent do you follow them up?
   – What have you learned from any follow up?
   – How has the learning modified your approach subsequently?

45

13. What features of your present interviewing performance would you like to improve?

Purpose

14. What is the purpose of the interview?

    - To obtain information?

      • To assess depth/extent of knowledge/skills/attitudes?
      • To decide suitability for a particular occupation/traineeship?

    - To give information?

      • To help the individual consider available options and make a choice?
      • To help the individual to help himself/herself?

    - To enhance your reputation as a caring/helpful/concerned individual/department/organization?
    - Or what?

15. What do you want/hope to achieve?

16. What does the individual want/hope to achieve?

17. What *should* be achieved? Who should decide?

18. In view of the possible purposes, is an interview the best way? The only way? The right way?

19. What evidence have you from past experience which may have a bearing on the present situation?

20. In relation to selection interviews, for instance, have you considered using:

    - Trainability tests?
    - Other vocational assessment procedures?

21. Is an interview appropriate? Are you sure?

Information

22. What information do you need before the interview?

    - Do you have it?

- If so, have you studied it?
- If not, how could a lack affect the outcome?

- Should the interview be postponed until you do have the necessary information?

Mental preparation

23. Are you prepared mentally for the interview?

   - Will you devote *all* your attention to it?
   - What changes/modifications to your present approach should be introduced this time?
   - What relationship should you establish?
   - Are you *really* prepared to listen?
   - What types of question will you use to achieve the purpose(s) of the interview?
   - How much talking should you do/should the individual do?
   - Will you suspend judgement/avoid jumping to conclusions?

Physical preparation

24. Are facilities for the interview appropriate?

   - Temperature?
   - Lighting?
   - Seating?
   - Privacy?
   - No interruptions?

Timing

25. Have you agreed a specific time for the interview? Do you intend to stick to it? If not, why?
   Remember: lateness may be perceived as discourtesy or lack of interest.

The interview itself

26. What structure should the interview take? Which elements of those shown in Figure 12.1 require particular attention?

Welcome
Put at ease
Clarify/agree the purpose/scope
Outline/agree sequence

Obtaining information	Giving information	Clarifying options
Keep purpose in mind	Keep purpose in mind	Keep purpose in mind
Maintain attitude of neutrality	Outline prospects and opportunities	Maintain attitude of neutrality
Encourage individual to talk	Clarify personal responsibility	Avoid imposing own standards/criticizing
Guide discussion unobtrusively	Ensure understanding	Listen actively
Elicit information/facts/opinions		Use the 'reflection' technique
Ask questions sensitively		'Wait out' pauses
Listen to what is said		Prompt consideration of *all* opinions
Listen between the lines		Allow individual to make own choice
Don't talk too much (20:80?)		
Encourage mutual understanding		

Parting
Be positive
Be courteous
Indicate/agree proposed action

Figure 12.1   The structure of an interview

Results

27. Has the interview achieved its purpose(s)? How do you know?

     – Are you happy?
     – Is the individual happy?
     – Was mutual understanding achieved?
     – Was there a practical/constructive/positive outcome?

28. What has been learned this time which will be of benefit for the future?

29. In what other ways will you ensure that any future interview is not damaging, either to your reputation, the reputation of the organization you represent, or the individual's future?

13 Introducing new employees

New recruits left to find out for themselves what they need to know are more likely to seek new pastures during their initial period of employment. This is known as the 'induction crisis'. Its impact may be assessed by implementing systematic induction procedures for all newcomers to the organization.

1. How do you rate the quality of introduction received by new employees to your organization?

2. Is it as effective as you would like? To what extent may the following factors indicate a deficiency in the process?

Background indicators

Staff turnover

3. What are the rates of staff turnover by different categories (age, department, function, etc.) for new employees?
   - What is the new employee survival index?
   - Is this figure acceptable? By what criteria?

Faulty work

4. What are the rates of scrap, rework, waste? Are these and other indicators of efficiency (and effectiveness) examined regularly in relation to new employees? Are these indicators acted on? Are you sure?

The learning curve

5. From a different perspective: how long does it take for new employees in various categories to become integrated into the organization? To reach an acceptable level of performance? Is the time taken to become fully experienced acceptable?

Health and safety

6. What is the accident frequency rate for new employees? How does the new employee sickness and absenteeism rate compare with that for longer-serving employees?

7. Have the causes behind these figures been considered in detail?

Management responsibility

8. Do members of management recognize the importance of effective induction procedures? If not, why? What should be done to rectify the situation? When? By whom?

9. Who has overall responsibility for effective induction in your organization? Specific responsibility? What role should the immediate supervisor of a new employee play in induction? Who else is involved in ensuring that the new employee receives a positive impression of the organization during the first few days/weeks of employment?

    – Should the responsibility be written into every supervisor's/manager's job description?

Introducing new employees: the practical implications

Operating a formal programme

10. If the answers to any of the above questions indicate a deficiency in approach, has the possibility of introducing/developing a formal induction programme been considered?

11. Are there sufficient new employees at any one time to mount a formal programme?

    – If so, how long should it last?
    – When should it be held?

- Immediately on joining?
- Or at a later date?
- Have the implications of holding it later been fully considered?

– Where should it be held?

- Is the environment really suitable for the purpose?

12. Have the questions to which new employees will probably want answers been considered in detail? Is it accepted that the following questions underpin any induction programme?

– What does the organization expect of me?
– What can I expect from the organization?
– Where do I fit in?

13. Which of the topics in Figure 13.1, and others not mentioned there, should be included?

– Has the proposed programme content been thought through?
– How have the priorities for including particular topics been set? For instance, should a session on handling techniques be included in view of the proportion of accidents attributable to this cause?
– Will the programme structure recognize the new employees as adults? Will sufficient time be made available for questions after each session?

14. Who should cover what topics?

– Will a senior manager introduce the programme to emphasize the importance accorded to it by management?
– Are the proposed speakers competent?
– Will back-up speakers be held in readiness in case of illness etc?

15. What aids to learning should be included in the programme?

– What visual aids will be used? Will these aids support the image of the organization you wish to project?
– What printed material will be distributed? Does it present a pro-gressive view of the organization? Is it suitably packaged? How does it relate to material already given to the new employee on engagement?

16. What evaluation/follow-up procedures should there be to ensure on-going effectiveness?

– Who should be involved?

– What would be the most effective way of evaluating the worth of the programme? On what time-scale?

17. Who should be responsible for implementing, developing and controlling such a formal programme?

Individual programmes

18. If there are insufficient new starters to mount formal programmes, do individual supervisors/managers induct their new staff effectively? How do you know?

19. Have all supervisors/managers undergone training in:

– The importance of effective induction?
– How to induct new starters?
– The topics which should be covered?

The organization	The employee: personal rights, responsibilities and benefits

Background
Development
Products/processes/services
Markets
Locations
Number of employees
Organization
Mission
The future
	Rights
	Wage/salary system
	– payment
	– additional payments
	  • bonuses
	  • differentials
	– incentives
	– deductions
	– loans
	– savings schemes
	– sickness

Geographical layout Departments Services Facilities Car parking	Pension arrangements Long-service awards Protective clothing Consultation Equality of opportunities
Policies Personnel Industrial relations Training and development Health and safety	Other rights under the law Further education/training *Responsibilities* Sickness

Figure 13.1 Topics relevant to an induction programme

The organization	The employee: personal rights, responsibilities and benefits
Communications	– self-certification
Data protection	– notification
Others important to your	– further certification
organization	Hours
	– clocking
Rules, regulations, procedures	– overtime
Works/office rules	– weekend working
Disciplinary procedure	– shift arrangements
Grievance procedure	– flexitime
Check off	– lateness
Notification of changes in personal	Health, safety, fire prevention
data	– personal responsibilities
Protection of organization's	– fire drills
assets	– evacuation procedures
Safeguarding of information	– good housekeeping
	– special hazards
Receiving division/department	*Benefits*
What it makes	Holidays
Service it provides	– bank, annual
Technical terms	– relation to length of service
Organization	Services
Employee representation	– first aid, medical
– safety	– private health insurance
– union	– cafeteria, restaurant
– other	Sports and social activities
Relationships	– clubs, societies
Consultation arrangements	Preferential purchases
Standards	– inside organization, in locality
Particular hazards	

Figure 13.1   concluded

20. When did they receive their training? What booster training may be needed now?

21. Has the introduction of a standard 'induction checklist' (see Figure 13.1 for possible topics) been considered to ensure uniformity of approach? (If not, what action is indicated? When? By whom? Could the layout shown in Figure 13.2 be useful?

Name: Department:				Date joined:
Topic	Item covered (✔)	Date	By Name	Title
1. 2. 3. etc.				

Figure 13.2　Example of a layout for an induction checklist

Follow-up

22. Whether the induction is formal or informal, what follow-up should be implemented?

  − Do you recognize that the impact of any initial induction may be lost if 'on-the-job' training practices are not of comparable quality?
  − Are those experienced staff involved in on-the-job training fully trained themselves for the role? Are you sure?

23. Has the idea of appointing individual mentors for new employees been considered for the first few weeks (or months) of employment?

Review

24. When was the last time employees with six to nine months' service were asked for their views on their introduction to the organization? Were the comments acted on? Is it time the exercise was carried out again? If the question has never been asked, what does this indicate about the probable quality of the introduction?

14 Letter writing

Writing letters was once considered an art and many books of letters written by famous people or notable exponents of that art have been published. In the business world, there is no place for literary artifice but letter writing remains an important part of business communications. Every letter deserves careful thought and planning before putting pen to paper or reaching for the keyboard or dictating machine. It takes time – but this is amply rewarded in the time saved as a result.

Intention

1. Have you analysed why a letter is necessary? Is it to:

    - Inform?
    - Instruct?
    - Explain?
    - Persuade?
    - Or what?

2. Can you express your purpose in a short, crisp phrase? Will you keep it in the forefront of your mind while writing/dictating?

Sense

3. What ideas/facts/arguments support your purpose? Have you considered what your reader must know by asking yourself the following questions?

    - What?
    - When?

- Where?
- How?
- Why?

Have you listed the important ideas your letter must express?

4. Can you write your letter in a pattern familiar to your reader? As narrative, dealing with events chronologically? As a reasoned argument, on a pattern of cause and effect? As description? Or what?

5. Have you arranged your ideas in order so that you are able to take your reader step-by-step with you as you write?

6. Have you taken care to move into your main subject/purpose without unnecessary conversational phrases?

7. Will you follow these basic rules:

   - Paragraphs: Will each paragraph deal with a single topic only?
   - Sentences: Will sentences be kept short? And not overloaded with ideas?
   - Words: Will short words and plain everyday language be used as far as possible? Will abstractions be avoided?

Feeling

8. Have you considered whether your communication can be made effectively in a factual way bleached of any emotion? Or whether the feelings of the reader will be involved?

9. Do you ensure that, whenever necessary, your organization's concern, interest, desires or other feelings about the subject are conveyed with tact and fairness? Do you make a positive effort to obtain and preserve the goodwill of your reader?

10. Do you also avoid the use of words which can take on colour by association? (For example, a 'skilled operator' in one context can imply praise; in another, condemnation.)

Tone

11. What will be the tone of your letter? Formal? Or informal? Do you use the informal approach whenever possible? And do you remember not to mix the styles?

12. What will be the opening/ending of your letter? Will it be: Dear Sir? Dear Mr Smith? Dear John? Yours faithfully? Yours truly? Yours sincerely? Yours ever?

13. If you are drafting an informal letter for someone else to sign, will you check his/her style and try to write in harmony with it?

14. Do you avoid the conscious or unconscious use of 'loaded' words and phrases? (For example: 'You did not understand'; 'You allege'; 'You overlooked'.)

15. If you have to refuse a request, do you remember to be tactful?

16. If the letter is important to you or your reader, do you take time for reflection or ask a colleague to read it before finally signing it?

17. Do you always ask yourself how *you* would react to the letter?

15   Listening

To listen to, and not merely to hear, what customers, colleagues and other staff members say is a vital skill. It is easy to avoid listening whether with your mind, or body, or both. To attend psychologically and physically involves effort: but it is worthwhile.

Preliminary diagnosis

1. To what extent would you agree that your ability to listen effectively has a serious impact on your job performance? On relationships at home? On contacts elsewhere? . . . and, perhaps most importantly, on you as a person?

2. How many hours of formal training in listening skills have you undertaken as an adult?

    –   What does your answer suggest about the likely level of your skill in this respect?

3. When was the last time you read an article or book on the subject of listening?

    –   What impact did your reading have on your skills as a listener? How do you know?

4. How would you currently rate your skill at asking questions? At listening effectively to the answers your questions generate (rather than merely hearing them)? Remember: asking questions and listening to the answers represent different sides of the same coin. Rate each skill on a scale from 1 (lowest) to 100 (highest).

5. How would those closest to you respond to the previous question? How would your colleagues respond? Your acquaintances?

   – Would the responses differ?
   – How would you account for any differences between their responses? Or similarities? Between their responses and yours?

Proposed action

6. How far do your answers to all the previous questions suggest that you could develop/extend your listening skills?

   – If your answer is 'not at all', are you sure that your responses have been accurate?
   – Are you fully aware of the many elements which contribute to a genuine ability to listen?

     • If not, what action is indicated?
     • If so, which particular elements will you concentrate on? Which of those listed in Figure 15.1 would repay particular attention?

7. Now review your proposed actions. What other action is necessary to ensure that your good intentions are implemented sucessfully? And monitored periodically? (How will you check your progress?)

8. What are the development implications of these questions for every other manager in your organization? For other employees?

   – Should every supervisor/management training programme con- ducted within your organization emphasize the crucial necessity for effective listening at every level? How can you establish the need? And then meet that need?

9. Over what time-scale would any action be appropriate?

10. What are you actually going to do, both personally and on behalf of your organization, on this topic during the rest of this week? Next week? And thereafter?

Some contributory elements	Current skill level low/ moderate/ high	Action?	Help needed from . . .	Time frame (action completed by)	Criteria for success
Physical attending (Listening with your body) – Staying relatively relaxed – Maintaining reasonable eye contact – Looking interested in what is being said – Keeping still (avoiding fidgeting) – Facing the speaker					
Pyschological attending (Listening with your mind) – Remaining neutral (keeping an open mind; not pre-judging) – Avoiding the mental (and spoken) 'Yes, but . . .' – Not interrupting in other ways (e.g. answering your own questions) – Not reacting to emotional words – Listening for the theme in what is said, not just the 'facts' – Listening 'between the lines' to the speaker's tone of voice – Weighing the evidence (evaluating content rather than how it is said) – Interpreting the speaker's non-verbal signals sensitively – Asking questions to ensure understanding – Not avoiding 'difficult' topics – Concentrating (resisting distractions)					

Figure 15.1   Developing your listening skills: an action plan

61

16 Making changes at work

It is tempting to believe that others will recognize and readily accept changes to established working practices – the advantages are self-evident, to you at least. Nevertheless, the successful introduction of changes at work depends on detailed planning and on consultation with everyone likely to be affected.

The proposed change

1. What is the precise nature of the change?

    – Why is it necessary?
    – What is wrong with what happens now?
    – How can the change be justified?

2. Compared with the present situation, what will be the advantage of the change? From whose point of view?

    – What will be the benefits?

      • For others? For you?

3. What are the short/medium/long-term objectives you wish to achieve?

    – Have you specified the success criteria in measurable terms?

      • Quality: How well?
      • Quantity: How much?
      • Cost: At what price?
      • Time: How soon?

4. When, specifically, would you prefer the change to take place? Over what time-scale?

    – Why at that time? Over that period?

        • Are you sure you are not trying to push the change through too quickly?
        • Will the groundwork have been completed effectively?
        • Will people be ready for the change when it happens?

5. Have you considered the possible disadvantages fully?

    – What industrial relations issues may be involved?

        • What may have been offered in exchange for acceptance of the change?

    – What degree of contingency planning will be necessary?
    – How much could it cost if things go wrong?
    – How far could the costs of the change increase if unchecked?
    – What degree of risk is involved compared with the intended return? Is that acceptable?
    – What could happen if people do not co-operate, particularly as a result of poor communication?
    – In brief, have you given sufficient thought to these aspects? And, in particular, to the 'people' element?

6. What training will be required before, and during, the change?

    – Will the need for training be accepted? By all concerned?
    – What type of training is involved? Initial/booster/retraining?
    – Can it be provided internally? Or will external resources be necessary?
    – How much will it cost?

7. Do your objectives require revision in the light of your answers to these questions?

    – Would a more modest change be appropriate? More realistic? More acceptable?

Consulting those affected

8. Why should people accept the change?

    – Have you considered the consequences of the proposal *fully* from their point of view?
    – What are the benefits for them? Is this really sufficient to win their acceptance?

9. What, specifically, can you do to ensure that everyone understands the proposal?

    –   Will you provide all those concerned with full background information?

10. Will the proposed change be considered with them?

    –   Will you consult *all* those who will be affected?

        •   If not, why not? Can you justify keeping people in the dark? Are you sure?

11. If you propose to 'sell' the change to them, how far may the proposal be seen as a threat, both individually and collectively?

    –   Do you recognize that this may be the key issue?
    –   How do you propose to deal with these perceived threats?
    –   Who are the opinion leaders?

        •   What will be the best strategy for convincing them?

    –   Have you considered how easily such an approach might backfire on you?

12. Is the climate right to involve people fully in deciding the particular parameters of the change?

    –   Do you accept that there is a close relationship between involvement and subsequent commitment?
    –   Are you prepared for criticism of your own preferred approach to the change?
    –   Are you sufficiently open-minded to heed suggestions and incorporate them in the proposal as appropriate?
    –   Are you clear about your own motives in proposing the change?

        •   What do you want to achieve from it, personally?
        •   What will others see you as wanting to achieve from it?

13. What effect has the consultation process had on your original objectives? Do they need further modification?

Introducing the change

14. Once agreement has been reached on introducing the change, how will it be implemented?

    –   What resources will be involved? Will these be sufficient?

- What constraints will apply? Are they recognized by all concerned?
- Are the contingency plans ready? Could they be brought into effect immediately, if necessary?
- How will progress towards the target be monitored?

15. Do all concerned know what part they are to play in the change?

   - Does everyone know who will do what, why, where, when and how to implement the change?

16. What existing communication lines can be used? What new ones will need to be set up?

   - Are individual authorities and responsibilities clearly understood?
   - Are interim reporting procedures required?
   - Should a steering group be set up?

      • What should the membership be?
      • How often should the group meet?
      • For how long should it meet?

17. How will the new situation be stabilized?

   - For how long should it be monitored? Who should decide? In consultation with who else?
   - How easy would it be for the previous situation to reassert itself? What can be done to prevent this?

Follow-up

18. Has the situation improved?

   - How much better is it now? From whose point of view?
   - Have you sought the views of all those involved?

      • How do they really feel?

   - Have your objectives been achieved?
   - What other unintended results has the change produced?

19. Did you approach the change in the most effective way?

   - What have you learned during the planning, execution and monitoring stages of the change for next time?

      • About yourself?
      • About others?

20. Was there appropriate emphasis on the human implications of the change, and not merely on the technical details?

    – Were the human consequences foreseen?

21. As somebody once said: 'There is no such thing as a technical change without a social effect.' What have been the social effects of this particular change? If they have not been wholly positive, what more needs to be done? When? By whom?

17　Managing stress

Stress is what happens to people when they believe they must cope but are not sure they can. Those who are suffering from stress may react to the symptoms in different ways, although once on the downward spiral many people find it increasingly difficult to combat stress. Stress is no respecter of persons; a senior manager may suffer in the same way as a junior staff member.

We all have our own personal stress threshold which can be crossed at any time. Often the point of transition is not even recognized. Identifying your own stressors will enable you to plan and implement appropriate action.

Analysing your personal stress factors

Within yourself

1. To what extent do you worry about your work?

2. Are you happy in your job? Or are minor issues assuming significance at the moment?

3. To what extent do you believe your personality matches your job?

Within your job

4. How far does your job involve unscheduled interruptions over which you have little control?

   – How unpredictable is your work schedule? For this week? For this month? For this year?

5. What 'time span of control' applies to your job? How soon can you be called to account for the decisions you make?

6. If you were to make a mistake, how serious would it be? What would be the repercussions for you personally? For your job? For other people?

   – Are people's health and safety in danger from the decisions you make?
   – Could their view of themselves be under threat from your decisions? Are they being made to feel inadequate?
   – Would any mistake make you feel inadequate?

7. Do you work irregular hours? Shift work? A disruptive pattern of work? Or in the evenings? Is your work itself dangerous?

The interface between home and work

8. To what extent do you take work home with you? Occasionally? Or regularly?

9. Can you 'switch off' when you leave work?

   – Do you think about work at home? Or about home at work? To what extent in either case?
   – Can you think about your home at work? Do you? Should you?
   – How far might you be torn between home and work? Does any conflict make you feel guilty?

Changes in circumstances

10. Have you changed your job recently? Or taken on new responsibilities? Or even been involved in an important business readjustment (for example, a merger or reorganization)?

11. Have there been any significant changes in your relationships with colleagues in the recent past? With more senior management? With other staff?

12. What changes, if any, have there been in your personal relationship with those close to you? Is this causing any 'problems' currently?

    – Have any comments been made about your moods? Approachability? About not doing things which need to be done? About your unwillingness or inability to make decisions? About being 'wrapped up in yourself'? Or about your lack of concentration?

13. Have you had to readjust to changed domestic circumstances within the past year?

   – Retirement of someone close to you?
   – Children leaving home?
   – Becoming a grandparent?
   – Divorce or separation?
   – Someone close returning to work or changing employment?
   – Moving home?
   – Suffering a bereavement?
   – Having an addition to the family?

14. How far are you worried about your personal finances?

   – Have you taken on any serious financial responsibilities recently?
   – Have your financial circumstances changed in any other way in the past few months? How? Is it bothering you?

15. Do you have any worries currently about your health or that of any people close to you?

   – Have you noticed any minor changes recently in your own condition (for instance, headaches) when you are under pressure?
   – Are you overweight? Or even underweight?
   – Do you smoke or drink too much? Or depend on tablets to keep you going through the day?
   – Do you suffer from any longer-term health problems which may be aggravated by your 'worries'?

16. Do your answers to any of these questions suggest that stress may be a more significant part of your life than it should be?

17. To what extent would you like to do something positive about the situation? If not, could this be part of the problem? Or do you believe the pay-off might not be worth the effort? How sure can you be?

Remember: Activity is not necessarily action!

Coping with stress

18. What action could you take to control your life more effectively? To reduce your current stress reactions?

19. Which of the following possibilities may be particularly appropriate for you?

Making decisions

20. Are your work and domestic decisions thought through effectively?

   – Are you sufficiently systematic in your decision making?
   – What are your work goals currently? Your domestic goals?
   – Do you review the alternative courses of action open to you before deciding what to do? Or do you rationalize your actions after the event?
   – Have you got your priorities right?
   – Would it be worth reviewing your 'must do', 'should do' and 'could do' priorities? Both at work and at home?
   – Do your priorities reflect current commitments?
   – When you do achieve success do you feel a sense of pride?

Managing your time

21. How well do you manage your time currently?

   – Do you tend to put off the important things which need to be done? Do you procrastinate and do the unimportant but interesting things first?
   – Do you give yourself sufficient time to think? Are you sure?
   – How often do you have difficulties in meeting deadlines? In doing other things you have promised to do at home?
   – Are you spending too much time on detail at work? And squandering time at home?
   – Are you dealing with the most important and pressing issues first? In both environments?

22. Would it be worth preparing a realistic 'to do' list for action in the next seven days?

   – How does the list compare with your answers to the previous question? What action, if any, does your answer suggest?
   – Does the list show how you are proposing to break out of your own personal stress cycle?
   – Are there any items on the 'to do' list which involve helping other people control/reduce their own stress levels? Should there be?
   – How will you monitor progress against the lists you prepare in the future? Will you actually do so? Are you sure?

Your personal values

23. What are the most important things in your life? The most important relationships?

    – How often do you tend to forget your answers?
    – How important are the relationships to you?
    – What are your true priorities?

24. In view of your answers to these questions, is your perspective on both work and home realistic? Is the balance right for you? For those close to you? Are you putting all your eggs in one basket?

25. What more could you do to redress the balance? Even if you are coping reasonably well with stress at the moment, are you doing all you can to prevent it happening? Are you sure?

Preventing stress

26. How well do you know yourself?

    – Do you know what is likely to cause you undue pressure?
    – Are you aware when you are under pressure from different sources?

    • Particular individuals?
    • Particular work situations?
    • Particular domestic situations?

    – Is your initial reaction fight? Or flight? What can you do to become more assertive?
    – Are you comfortable in your preferred stance in different situations? Would you like to change? How? Would it help you to cope better with any stress?

27. How much exercise do you take? Is that enough?

    – What more could you do to improve your physical health?
    – What more could you do to think positively? To think about your good qualities and achievements?
    – Are you aware that such action will help to prevent stress?

28. Do you maintain a sensible and balanced diet? Do you eat healthily? How do you know?

    – In general terms, are you looking after yourself?

29.   What is your favourite method of relaxing? What other methods do you use?

    –   Is it possible that you are mistaking inactivity for relaxation?
    –   Do you sleep too much? Or not enough?
    –   Does your self-view allow you to try seemingly novel approaches to relaxation?
    –   How much do you know about techniques such as meditation and yoga?

30.   Do you have a few close friends? Or a wide circle of acquaintances?

    –   Can you really talk problems through with these people?
    –   Or are your problems being 'bottled up'?

31.   What actions do your answers to the last five questions suggest? Are you genuinely prepared to think through your responses? And do something positive about the situation?

32.   Can you justify inaction? Are you sure? To what extent could your response be a rationalization?

33.   Where will you go from here? What feelings have these questions prompted in you?

18 Managing your boss

The way you relate to your boss at work probably affects your whole life. If you feel positive about the relationship, your job seems more satisfying and worthwhile – your home life feels better, too. On the other hand, if the relationship is less positive, the reverse will apply: your more negative feelings will spill over into your life outside work.

How you get on together is critical. And whatever the flavour of the relationship with your boss at the moment, the chances are that it can be improved. Such improvement starts with a cool look at both yourself and your boss: your strengths, your weaknesses, your personalities and your skills. This assessment provides a framework within which the relationship may be developed.

This checklist focuses on the relationship as it is now and what it might become. It cannot tell you what to do but it will help you decide what needs to be done. Whether you use it as a precision tool rather than as a blunt instrument is up to you.

1. How effective is your boss in managing your colleagues? In managing you?

Mark your assessment at the appropriate point on the line shown below

1_____ 100

Very poor   Excellent

Figure 18.1 Your assessment of your relationship with your boss

2. In general terms, how do your colleagues get on with your boss? How do you?

   – Can you score just how well you personally get on, using the scale illustrated in Figure 18.1?

3. What would your boss answer if asked how he/she gets on with you?

   – Can you score the predicted response on the same horizontal line shown in Figure 18.1?

4. Now reflect on your own self-assessment, and on the assessment of how your own boss would respond.

   – What events were you thinking of particularly which have contributed to the assessments? From your point of view? From that of your boss?
   – What has gone well over the past twelve months and helped to extend the relationship? What has gone less well? In both cases, why?
   – What is your boss contributing currently to your joint relationship?
   – What are you contributing?
   – What do your answers tell you about the flavour of the relationship?

5. To what extent are you both contributing equally to a worthwhile working relationship?

   – How can you be sure your response is accurate?

6. What tasks have you performed particularly well in the past year? What tasks, if any, have not been performed as well?

   – Which elements of your job performance have caused you to feel particularly satisfied in the same period?
   – Which elements have resulted in a lack of satisfaction?
   – To what extent is your boss involved in, or even responsible for, your assessments?

     • Has your boss contributed to your feelings of satisfaction?
     • Or does the reverse apply?
     • In either case, what has been the impact of your boss on your feelings?

7. How far has negotiation of your role (or lack of it) with your boss over the past year contributed to your feelings? What effect has this had on your job satisfaction? Or lack of it?

8. Reflecting again on events during the past year, how often has your

boss complimented you on your performance? And how often has your performance been criticized by your boss?

- What were the origins of these compliments and/or criticisms?
- Were the comments, whatever their forms, justified in your view? What is the basis for your response?
- What are the stronger points of your performance as far as your boss is concerned?
- What are your perceived weaknesses?

9. Within your job do you operate against periodically agreed, clearly defined objectives?

- To what extent might your response be contributing to your previous answers? Should it be contributing? Or not?

10. To what degree has your boss commented in any way, during the past year, on aspects of your personality in relation to your job performance?

- If such comments have been made, do you consider them to have been fair at the time they were made?

    • To what extent may such past comments be affecting your performance now?
    • Have the comments been accommodated? Or could they be causing a confirming measure of pride? Or resentment?

11. What do your answers tell you about the kind of comments you may, even inadvertently, still be seeking, or receiving, from your boss in the relationship?

Current situation

12. What do your answers to the previous questions tell you about the state of your relationship now with your boss? Can you locate the principal focus of the relationship within the quadrant illustrated in Figure 18.2? (Remember: a mix of both positive and negative feelings may well contribute to your overall assessment.)

13. Having again reflected on your assessment, what are you doing currently to consolidate the stronger elements of the relationship? And to minimize, or even eradicate, the weaker points?

- What does your answer suggest about your commitment to developing your job performance? And to developing the relationship with your boss?

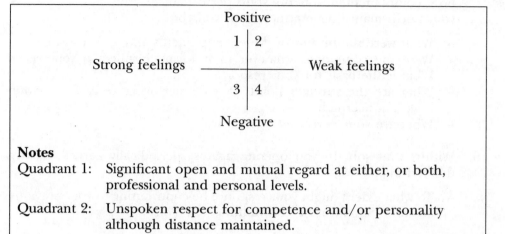

Notes

Quadrant 1: Significant open and mutual regard at either, or both, professional and personal levels.

Quadrant 2: Unspoken respect for competence and/or personality although distance maintained.

Quadrant 3: Marked, probably mutual, antipathy which may be the result of continuing criticism or indirect adverse feedback on the one side, and perceived incompetence on the other.

Quadrant 4: Probable lack of understanding about what each does and how each operates. Tendence of either to 'slap' the other in passing, but otherwise to remain at a distance.

Figure 18.2   Present relationship

14. What more could you be doing now to improve your performance? And the relationship?

    – Have you examined the present situation in sufficient detail to plan what could be done? What needs to be done? (See, for instance, Figure 18.3.)

15. How well do you really know your boss?

    – Would a deeper knowledge and understanding assist you in developing the relationship?
    – What do you know about your boss now?

16. Complete the skeleton assessment illustrated in Figure 18.4, both in terms of your perceptions of your boss's current skills, and behaviour, and in terms of any changes you would wish your boss to make? (Use each of the four columns numbered '1'.) Complete the assessment now.

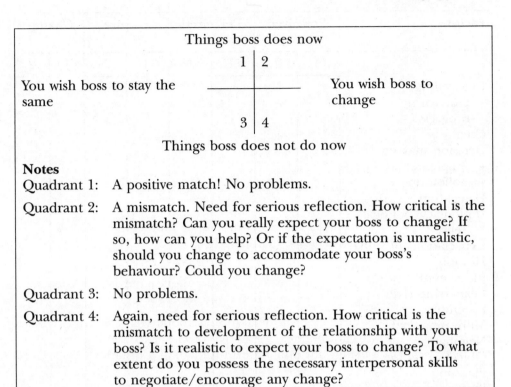

Things boss does now

You wish boss to stay the same

You wish boss to change

Things boss does not do now

Notes

Quadrant 1: A positive match! No problems.

Quadrant 2: A mismatch. Need for serious reflection. How critical is the mismatch? Can you really expect your boss to change? If so, how can you help? Or if the expectation is unrealistic, should you change to accommodate your boss's behaviour? Could you change?

Quadrant 3: No problems.

Quadrant 4: Again, need for serious reflection. How critical is the mismatch to development of the relationship with your boss? Is it realistic to expect your boss to change? To what extent do you possess the necessary interpersonal skills to negotiate/encourage any change?

Figure 18.3 Perceptions of boss's behaviour

Tick the appropriate column:

Factor	Perceived strength		Perceived weakness		Unsure		Change	
	1	2	1	2	1	2	1	2
Achievement orientation								
Assertiveness level								
Availability to staff								
Coaching and guidance								
Communication								
– oral								
– written								
Commitment								
Co-ordination								
Consultation								

Figure 18.4   Personal assessment

Factor	Perceived strength		Perceived weakness		Unsure		Change	
	1	2	1	2	1	2	1	2
Controlling/ monitoring progress								
Creativity								
Decision making								
– implementation								
– follow-up								
Delegation								
Diplomacy/political 'sense'								
Expectations of staff								
Honesty								
Judgement								
Leadership style								
Listening								
Motivating staff								
Negotiating								
Objective setting								
Planning								
Presentation								
Problem solving								
Reality, sense of								
Responsibility, acceptance of								
Risk taking								
Self-discipline								
Sensitivity to events								
Stability under pressure								
Staff development								
Supportiveness								
Team building								
Temperament								
Time management								
Thinking, maturity of								

Figure 18.4   continued

Factor	Perceived strength		Perceived weakness		Unsure		Change	
	1	2	1	2	1	2	1	2
Trustworthiness Vision Work capacity								
Other significant factors:								

Figure 18.4 concluded

17. Now repeat the exercise for yourself. Can you identify your own strengths and weaknesses, using the same factors? (Use each of the four columns numbered '2'.) Complete your self-assessment now.

18. Reviewing both your assessments, have you been objective?

    – Have you thought through the issues?
    – How can you be sure that your responses do not merely reflect a desire for an easy life? For increased autonomy without the concomitant need for increased productivity? For absence of any performance assessment?
    – What unwarranted assumptions might you have made?
    – To what extent might your boss produce a different assessment in answer to the same questions?
    – Would it be worth checking your self-perceptions, and your perceptions of your boss, with people (for example, colleagues) you trust and who know both of you?

19. What do both assessments tell you? Complete the skeleton summary shown in Figure 18.5.

    – Which *strengths* do you apparently possess in common with your boss?
    – Which *strengths* do you not possess in common?

      • Which does your boss possess?
      • Which do you have?

    – Which *weaknesses* do you apparently possess in common with your boss?
    – Which *weaknesses* do you not possess in common?

      • Which does your boss exhibit?
      • Which do you exhibit?

	Strengths	Weaknesses
Shared		
Yours, but not boss's		
Boss's, but not yours		

Figure 18.5 Summary of strengths and weaknesses

20. Which of the strengths both of you possess contribute particularly to your present relationship with your boss?

   – What thought could you give to consolidating these strengths?
   – What thought will you give?

21. Which of the strengths possessed by you, but not your boss, could also be used in developing the relationship?

22. And which of the weaknesses both of you possess could be detracting from your relationship?

   – Which are the critical weaknesses? Which appear to be having the most damaging impact on the relationship?
   – What could you do to improve the situation? What will you do?

23. Which weaknesses does your boss exhibit which you do not?

    – Is there any way in which you could compensate personally for particular weaknesses?
    – Are you prepared to consider such possible compensation in detail? If so, when will you think about it in concrete terms?

24. Which of the weaknesses you exhibit, which your boss does not, could be detracting disproportionately from the relationship?

    – In what ways could you lessen the impact of these weaknesses?

      • What are you doing now?
      • What more could you do?
      • Might it be worth seeking help from your boss?
      • What formal off-the-job training programme(s) may be appropriate?
      • What on-the-job coaching and guidance may also be particularly appropriate?

25. What does your summary analysis suggest?

    – How great is the overlap between your respective strengths? And weaknesses?
    – On how many items of your assessment of your boss were you unsure? And on your assessment of yourself? How significant is your response when considered against your summary analysis?
    – At what level would you rate your value to your boss at present?
    – What are the primary influences on your assessment?
    – How valuable are you?

26. How could you become more valuable to your boss? Do you want to?

    – Have you thought through the possible consequence of any increased value? In sufficient detail?

27. Do you truly want to extend the relationship?

    – If so, which particular factors in your assessment could repay closest attention over the next month? The following month? Thereafter?

28. Are you prepared to take 51 per cent of the responsibility for improving (extending) the relationship?

    – At a personal level, which of your perceived strengths would be worth consolidating? Which should be tackled first? How?
    – Which of your perceived weaknesses could/should be rectified? In what order? Again, how?
    – What action on your part would have a marked impact quickly?

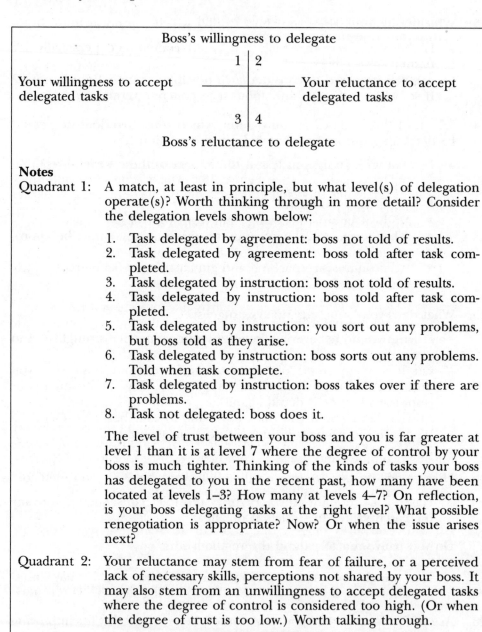

Notes

Quadrant 1: A match, at least in principle, but what level(s) of delegation operate(s)? Worth thinking through in more detail? Consider the delegation levels shown below:

1. Task delegated by agreement: boss not told of results.
2. Task delegated by agreement: boss told after task completed.
3. Task delegated by instruction: boss not told of results.
4. Task delegated by instruction: boss told after task completed.
5. Task delegated by instruction: you sort out any problems, but boss told as they arise.
6. Task delegated by instruction: boss sorts out any problems. Told when task complete.
7. Task delegated by instruction: boss takes over if there are problems.
8. Task not delegated: boss does it.

The level of trust between your boss and you is far greater at level 1 than it is at level 7 where the degree of control by your boss is much tighter. Thinking of the kinds of tasks your boss has delegated to you in the recent past, how many have been located at levels 1–3? How many at levels 4–7? On reflection, is your boss delegating tasks at the right level? What possible renegotiation is appropriate? Now? Or when the issue arises next?

Quadrant 2: Your reluctance may stem from fear of failure, or a perceived lack of necessary skills, perceptions not shared by your boss. It may also stem from an unwillingness to accept delegated tasks where the degree of control is considered too high. (Or when the degree of trust is too low.) Worth talking through.

Quadrant 3: Boss may not wish to 'let go' because of fear of takeover. Such fear may be shown in distrust. Again, worth consultation?

Quadrant 4: A total mismatch. Shortcomings on both sides? Not a question of whether consultation is necessary, but when!

Figure 18.6 Delegation: willingness/reluctance

29. Considering your job as a whole, would another positive move be to clarify your role further with your boss?

     – Would another be to negotiate, or re-negotiate, elements of your role for the future?

30. What other issues in the relationship could and should be tackled? When?

     – For instance, are you happy with the forms and degree of delegation to you by your boss? (See Figure 18.6 which represents one quick way of analysing this element, itself one of those illustrated earlier in Figure 18.4.)
     – Could your boss 'let go' rather more than at present? Or is there a genuine match, a willingness to offer, and a willingness to accept, delegated tasks? Or is there a reluctance on either side? If so, why? Is further analysis required before any action is taken?

31. Bearing in mind that your boss is hardly likely to change just because you may wish it, what will be your priorities for the future? Your specific objectives? Would it be worth preparing an action plan similar to that illustrated in Figure 18.7?

32. Will your objectives be realistic? And achievable? And properly evaluated once achieved? Remember: particular objectives can be simple, as well as more complex. It may be that simply stopping doing something (spending too much time in casual conversation with colleagues, missing deadlines, and the like) could have a disproportionately positive impact. Aim for success in the simple objectives first and, once achieved, check regularly for possible slippage. Try to make success a habit.

33. Do your objectives suggest that you will be managing your boss? Or perhaps more realistically, managing with your boss?

     – Are you sure that you will not be attempting to manipulate your boss? Do you recognize the possible consequences of such an approach?
     – Will you truly be using the situation to your mutual advantage?
     – Will you also be helping to improve yourself? Or merely to improve your situation from your own selfish point of view?
     – Are you proposing to be part of a solution? Or will you continue to be part of a problem?
     – Will you be proactive? Or reactive?

Broad focus of action (aims)	Objectives	To be achieved by (date) (now, soon, sometime?)
Must		
Should		
Could		

Figure 18.7   Action plan

34.   What do your answers say about you? Are you comfortable with your response? If so, are you likely to do anything?

35.   What are your motives in wanting to manage more effectively with your boss?

   –   Do you want to extend the relationship? For professional reasons? For personal reasons? Or other reasons? If so, which?
   –   Can you justify your reading of this checklist?

36.   How often are you proposing to review any developments?

   –   When should you check progress against your objectives?

37.   At what point, if ever, will you discuss your analysis and proposals with your boss?

   –   Could discussion take place now?

    – If not, what does your response say about you? Your boss? Is this particular issue worth further reflection?

    – In any event how will any achievements be publicized? How can these achievements be made visible? To whom? To what extent should they?

38. Are you genuinely committed to your own development? Sufficiently proactive? And truly sensitive?

39. As a human resource development specialist are you ready for the challenge of assisting those involved to extend their own development? To become even more productive? And to gain a higher level of job satisfaction?

40. What do your answers suggest about your own future? Remember: bosses do not normally move on until successors have been developed. In your own situation, should the successor be you? Why?

19 Managing your time

Time is the most valuable resource at your disposal. It is also absolute. The time you have spent reading these words can never be relived; the moment has gone forever.

Making good use of your time requires a positive act of will, a self-discipline in planning the passing hours. The following questions have been designed to help you 'fine tune' your time usage.

Preliminary diagnosis

1. Are you managing your time as effectively as you might? Currently? Long term? At work? Elsewhere? Do you plan your life? Or does it have a tendency to plan you?

2. To what extent would you agree that any of the following could apply to you:

    - Missing deadlines?
    - Putting off things which you ought to do?
    - Spending too long on telephone calls you didn't start?
    - Having insufficient time to think?
    - Being unsure where your time goes?
    - Achieving less than you think your efforts deserve?
    - Feeling you have to say 'yes' to people?
    - Dealing personally with too many work crises?
    - Attempting to achieve perfection in tasks rather than excellence, and achieving neither?
    - Waiting for meetings which start late?
    - Indulging in lengthy evening 'naps'?
    - Failing to keep your promises on domestic tasks?

	Self		Others	
	Initiated	Controlled/ Monitored	Initiated	Controlled/ Monitored
At work				
Meetings				
With one person				
With small group				
With large group				
Telephone calls				
Started ⎫ work				
Received ⎬				
Started ⎫ non-work				
Received ⎭				
Dictation				
Report writing				
Reading				
Correspondence				
Professional update				
Thinking alone				
Travelling				
Other (specify):				
At home				
Telephone calls				
Started ⎫ work				
Received ⎬				
Started ⎫ non-work				
Received ⎭				
Writing				
Work originated				
Other				
Thinking alone				
Reading				
Work originated				
Professional update				
Other (specify):				
Entertaining/being entertained				
Watching TV/video				
Listening to radio/records/ tapes				
Other leisure activities (specify):				
Keeping fit				
Sleeping				
Other (specify):				

Figure 19.1   Current time investment (%)

- Arriving home late because of 'pressure of work'?
- Thinking too much about work problems at home?
- Thinking too much about home problems at work?
- Spending insufficient time with your family?
- Forgetting birthdays/anniversaries/other special dates?
- Spending too much time travelling?
- Regarding travelling time as 'dead' time?

3. Does the figure '168' mean anything to you? Or '8760'? Should these numbers mean anything?

4. Is time important to you? As it is the only absolute (irreversible) resource at your disposal, what are you planning to do in the next 365 days to extend your use of this time? To achieve more than you have to date?

5. What will you do in the next 24 hours? The next 168 (a week)? In the following 700 + (a month)? And in the 8760 hours which make up the next year from today?

Current time investment

6. How do you spend your time? What activities take up most of your time? What take up the remainder?

    - Can you identify and subsequently quantify in percentage terms, your relative time investment using Figure 19.1
    - If you cannot, what are you doing with your time? Should you start to log your time now so that you can establish what you are doing? Over the next week? Over the next month? A longer period?

7. What seems to be the primary emphasis of the time investment you make now? Just how much of your time is self-initiated and self-monitored? How much is initiated and controlled by others?

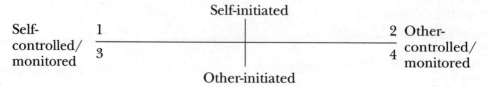

Figure 19.2   Quadrant: current time investment

8. Can you locate your relative time investment on the quadrant shown in Figure 19.2? (Your response will be 'clusters' of your responses to Figure 19.1.)

9. It is likely that most of your time spent at work is located in quadrant 4. It is now worth reflecting on how you could make additional space for yourself (expanding the time spent in quadrant 1)?

   – In this respect, what is your answer in relation to your time at home? And elsewhere?

10. How much of your total time investment is spent effectively (doing the right things) rather than merely efficiently (doing things right)? Can you locate the proportions of efficient and effective time on the quadrant shown in Figure 19.3?

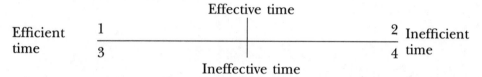

Figure 19.3   Quadrant: effective/efficient time investment

11. Are you the prime initiator/controller of your effective time investment? Or is it initiated/controlled by others? At work? At home? Elsewhere? What is your answer on your efficient time investment in the same three environments?

12. If you were to conduct a SWOT (Strengths, Weaknesses, Opportunities, Threats) analysis today of your total time investment, what would be your strengths? (Using your time both effectively and efficiently represents a strength. Such strength allows you to exploit time which would otherwise be wasted; it certainly represents an opportunity to achieve more. Using time ineffectively, or inefficiently, or both, represents a weakness which itself could constitute a threat, both now and in the future.) What would be your relative weaknesses? What specifically is your current position on time planning, usage and control? Can you locate your answers in Figure 19.4?

   – What do your answers suggest about ways in which you could use your strengths to further exploit opportunities? And the ways in which your relative weaknesses could constitute a threat to you if not dealt with positively? At work? At home? Elsewhere?

   – How do your answers compare with your current time investment?

Key area	(Tick (✔))			
	Strength	Weakness	Opportunity	Threat
Doing the right things: effective time investment				
1.				
2.				
3.				
4.				
5.				
6.				
7.				
8.				
9.				
10.				

Figure 19.4   Current time investment: a SWOT analysis

Key area	(Tick (✔)) Strength	Weakness	Opportunity	Threat
Doing things right: efficient time investment				
1.				
2.				
3.				
4.				
5.				
6.				
7.				
8.				
9.				
10.				

NOTE: The identification of strengths indicates opportunities for the future: building on current strengths creates future opportunities. The identification of current weaknesses on the other hand creates the opportunity for rectification in the future. If the opportunity is declined however, the weaknesses could well represent an increasing threat.

Personal notes arising from the SWOT analysis:

Date completed ....

Figure 19.4   concluded

Degree of urgency

	Now (most urgent)	Soon (urgent)	Sometime (less urgent)
Must (most important)	1.	2.	3.
Should (important)	2.	3.	4.
Could (less important)	3.	4.	5.

Degree of importance

Figure 19.5 Time investment matrix

13. Whatever the results of your analysis, are you prepared to act to increase the proportion of self-initiated/controlled *effective* time usage? Or will you succumb to paralysis-by-analysis? Will you act? Or react?

14. Having now considered the 'what?' and 'so what?' of managing your time effectively, will you accept the challenge? And deal purposefully with the last question of the trio: 'now what?'

An improvement strategy

15. Are you now in a position to prioritize, more effectively, your current commitments both at, and from, home and work, using the time investment matrix shown in Figure 19.5?

Feasibility	Is your proposed action realistic? Is it achievable? With or without help? What obstacles could prevent success? Can these obstacles be removed, with effort? What amount and quality of help will be necessary? Is it available now? Could the situation change? How will you accommodate any changes? At work? At home?
Suitability	Will achievement assist/promote personal productivity at work? If not, why have you included this item as a priority? Would it be worth considering both the direct *and* indirect impact of the item on your future productivity? Will achievement assist domestic harmony? Again, what will be the impact, both direct and indirect?
Acceptability	Does your proposed action meet with your own personal approval? If not, could it be that you are procrastinating? That you believe any 'problem' will solve itself, given time? That you are too busy in any event? Or that the degree of personal risk is unacceptable? Will your proposed action meet with domestic approval? If not, do priorities require renegotiation? Will the action meet with corporate approval? If not, might the degree of risk be unacceptable? Again, do priorities require renegotiation?

Figure 19.6 Your proposed actions: three critical dimensions

Factor	Degree of urgency			(Tick (✔)) Degree of importance			Details of action to be taken
	Now	Soon	Sometime	Must	Should	Could	
Controlling effect of personal stress on time usage							
Extending personal assertiveness (saying 'no' and meaning it)							
Modifying your availability							
Improving reading skill							
Using 'dead' time more effectively							
Extending your power of decision making							
Delegating more effectively							
Extending thinking time							
Developing relationships							
Other (specify):							

Figure 19.7 Extending personal competence

16.   Reviewing each of the items you have located in the various cells which constitute your time investment matrix, are you sure that the achievement of each item is feasible? And suitable? And also acceptable? (Remember: identifying the relative feasibility, suitability and

94

acceptability of the priorities you have identified is just as critical to success as identifying relative importance and urgency.) Some questions which may help to determine the impact of these three dimensions are shown in Figure 19.6.

In assessing the feasibility, suitability and acceptability of your judgement you may care to remember the words attributed to St Francis of Assisi: 'Grant me the courage to change those things which can be changed, the serenity to accept those things which cannot be changed . . . and the wisdom to know the difference.'

17. Reassessing now your answers to the personal SWOT analysis in question 12, what could you change in yourself to extend your own personal time-effectiveness in achieving your priorities? Which of the possibilities shown in Figure 19.7, amongst others, should you consider in detail now?

18. Can the points you have included in Figure 19.7 now be added to your time-investment matrix (Figure 19.5)?

19. What in total are you committing yourself to do? Over the next week? The next month? A longer period?

    – How will you ensure that your intentions (both plans and their monitoring) will be actioned effectively?
    – What else do you need to do to ensure success?
    – Will this checklist constitute a working document over the coming weeks? Or will it be quietly ignored?

20. Are you ready to make a genuine start on improving your time-management skills? And having started, how specifically will you keep going? Do you propose to consolidate any benefits arising from this commitment? What can you do to keep the impetus going?

20   Motivating your staff

The manager's job of achieving tasks through other people is always easier when morale is high and staff are well motivated. Maintaining good working relations and a high level of motivation requires above all a sound understanding of individual needs and attitudes. People are not produced from the same mould. The manager who appreciates and allows for differences in character and aptitude when handling individuals and the group will achieve greater motivation – and success.

1.   When carrying out your prime management tasks, do you place sufficient emphasis on motivating your staff?

2.   Do you ever tend to treat your staff as if they were all alike? Do you make special efforts to accommodate individual needs when communicating with them?

3.   Do you ever have to remind yourself that people react in terms of their own personality and experience? Do you treat your staff as if their reactions ought to be precisely the same as yours?

4.   During work planning, do you consider sufficiently people's likely reactions?

5.   Are you still treating your staff the same way now as you were twelve months ago? Why? Have you made sufficient allowance for changes in their – and your – attitudes, expectations, knowledge and skill?

6.   Do you recognize the needs and attitudes of both individuals and the group?

7.   What appear to be the main needs and attitudes of each of your people?

8. Where does each of them, in your judgement, fit into the following scales of needs/attitudes?

Identification, subjective thinking	——————————	Detachment, objective thinking
Knowledge, facts and figures	——————————	Faith, reassurance
Creativity, positive contribution	——————————	Destructiveness, sarcasm, negative attitude
Respect for authority, deference	——————————	Contempt, rebellion
Control, domination	——————————	Submission
Harmony, order	——————————	Contrasts, incongruity
Desire to consolidate	——————————	Desire to diversify
Tradition	——————————	Innovation
Affection, liking	——————————	Dislike, malice
Individualism	——————————	Conformity
Equality, levelling	——————————	Ranking, order
Rest, laziness	——————————	Activity
Security, caution	——————————	Risk, adventure
Collect, acquire	——————————	Give way, distribute

9. Are you sure you have judged the above needs and attitudes soundly?

10. Are these needs compatible with achievement of the job?

11. If they are not, what do you propose to do about rectifying the situation?

12. If you recognize individuals' needs and attitudes, do you adopt differing tactics in dealing with them? If not, why not? What is stopping you?

13. Do you adopt a policy of using individuals' strengths to get the job done? If not, why not? How does that reflect on your own motivation?

14. What plans have you for minimizing weaknesses (in attitude, skill or knowledge) among your staff? Do these plans include motivation on a cause–effect basis?

15. Do you accept that for most people achievement at work and recognition of a job well done are prime motivators of behaviour?

16. How does this point relate to your view of their ego and self-respect needs?

17. Do you accept that for some people self-fulfilment means fulfilment in their jobs?

18. Does this apply to any people in your department?

19. What, if anything, are you doing about it?

20. Have you considered the relative importance of the factors which make your staff act and react in the way they do?

21. When was the last time you read an article/book on the subject? Is your own knowledge up to date? How can you be sure?

22. If it isn't, what do you propose to do to rectify the situation?

21 Performance appraisal: The system

Performance appraisal can be defined as periodic, formal (i.e. written) evaluation of an employee's job performance which may serve a variety of purposes. Whilst there are nearly 30 appraisal methods to choose from, it should be understood that the final choice will communicate the value structure (the culture) of an organization. The utility of an appraisal programme, its purpose, its form, operation and reception are all issues which reflect organizational values.

Background considerations

1. What do the words 'performance appraisal' mean in your organization?

    - To top management?
    - To you?
    - To supervisors and managers at different levels?
    - To everyone else?

2. To what extent might the views differ? When was the last time a check was made?

3. Could anyone in your organization have made the following comments on performance appraisal?

    - It isn't needed: the good people are like the cream – they always rise to the top
    - It's just form-filling. Nothing ever happens
    - Doesn't it mean that annual get-together for the anointed?
    - Nothing to do with me
    - Going on the occasional course
    - Talking to the boss about what he thinks I haven't done

- Just another on-cost
- Yes, we ought to have some
- I ask for courses but nothing's ever happened
- You'll get on anyway if the managing director likes you
- It's a good idea but they don't know how to go about it
- It's something for the top people only – not the likes of you and me
- A farce, a complete farce!
- I spend far too much time on it and then haven't got enough for my real job
- A waste of time
- I won't ever get promoted, I'm too valuable where I am
- Appraisal? It's a joke!

4. How important is it for everyone in your organization to be clear about the meaning of performance appraisal and their own personal rights and responsibilities in relation to it? Are the aims of appraisal fully understood? Are you sure?

5. Should an evaluation of what happens now be conducted as a first step towards more effective performance appraisal?

6. If ever such an evaluation should take place, will the following issues be considered?

Aims

7. What are the aims or purposes of performance appraisal in your organization? Do they include:

   - Helping individuals to improve and extend their job performance?
   - Identifying current training needs?
   - Helping to prepare people for possible promotion by identifying longer-term development needs?
   - Ensuring that sufficient suitable people are available at all levels to meet the organization's management succession needs in the foreseeable future?

   If not, what *are* the aims of performance appraisal in your organization? Whatever they may be, are equality of opportunity and positive encouragement of self-development regarded as basic principles? Are the principles honoured and carried through into practice, by all concerned? If not, why not?

8. Taking the aims you have identified, are they too diffuse? Are there too

many? Are they realistic? Do they relate effectively to one another? Are they achievable? Are they achieved now? . . . How do you know?

9. Do the aims form part of a policy statement on performance appraisal?

   – Does everyone have a copy of this statement?
   – Is the personal responsibility of all supervisors and managers for helping their own staff to develop themselves clearly specified? Is it also written into every supervisory/management job description?
   – Are managers in no doubt that discharging this responsibility effectively is critical to their own personal success in the organization?

10. Is the policy derived from, and co-ordinated with, corporate business plans? If not, what does this imply about the effectiveness of your organization's approach?

11. Does the policy have the full approval and agreement of top management? If unions are involved, were they consulted and their agreement gained? If there is no policy statement, what should be done? By whom? How quickly?

The system

12. Does the system work?

   – How do you know?

     • How does it compare with the approach used elsewhere in your industry? Nationally?
     • If it does not compare favourably, why not? What should be done?
     • When was the last time an evaluation exercise was carried out? With what result?
     • Is the time ripe to carry out such an exercise again now?

13. How is performance appraised? How does the system operate?

   – Is performance assessed against pre-set objectives?

     • Are targets/standards of performance agreed for the review period? And subsequently assessed? By whom in the first instance? Is self-appraisal operated formally? If not, how can its absence be justified?

   – Or is performance assessed in a more general way?

     • If so, just how subjective is it? Is it really fair to those being

101

appraised? For instance, if personal qualities are rated, is the behaviour critical to the job? If not, why is it rated?
  - Are the ratings made by different managers comparable? How can you be sure? What possible action does your answer indicate?

- Does the system meet its aims? Does the documentation reflect the aims of the system? Are you sure? How do you know?

14. Are the shortcomings of a general approach to appraisal recognized fully?

    - Is the procedure used in your organization open to criticism?
    - Is it truly supportive of effective management action? Are you sure?
    - If not, what action is indicated?

15. Are all staff, at all levels, appraised? Is the system primarily concerned with existing managers, potential managers, or both?

    - If not both, why not? What is the justification? Does it genuinely hold water?
    - If so, how is a 'potential manager' defined? If the definition does not include all non-managerial employees, why not?

16. How often are staff appraised?

    - If it is more infrequently than once a year, why? What is the justification? Again, is that reasonable?
    - Or is it seen merely as a once-a-year activity without any follow-up in the intervening period?
    - Who is responsible for conducting the appraisal? If it is not the individual's immediate superior, why not?

17. Does everyone know exactly what their rights and responsibilities are in relation to the appraisal system?

    - Do they know what is expected of them? Are you sure?
    - Do people believe in it? Do they want to make it work or do they endure it? How do you know?

Individual involvement

18. Is each individual appraised:

    - Fully involved in the procedure?
    - Asked for comments on his/her performance, development wishes and career intentions on the appraisal form? Or, alternatively, on a 'self-appraisal' preparatory form?

- Shown his/her supervisor's written appraisal?
- Given the opportunity to comment further on this appraisal? On the form? At the interview, if there is one? Or both?
- Shown the comments of his/her senior manager?
- Given a copy of the form when finally completed, if requested?

If not, is the system as 'open' as it should be?

19. If the individual is not fully involved in the ways outlined above, why not? What is the justification for conducting the exercise in confidence? How can it be fair to all concerned?

    - How can people believe in it? Or make it work?
    - Is the time ripe for review?

Appraisal interviews

20. Are appraisal interviews an integral part of the programme?

    - If not, why not? How can such an absence be justified?
    - If so, are all supervisors and managers fully trained and competent to discharge this particular responsibility? Are you sure?

      • For example, is training in appraisal interviewing given to *all* newly-appointed supervisors and managers? In coaching and counselling techniques? *Before* they are expected to carry out the interviews? If not, why not? If so, what booster training may be necessary now?
      • How effective are the appraisal interviews in particular departments now? Are some better than others? Why are they better?
      • What action does your answer suggest?

21. To re-emphasize the point, are all those concerned in appraising staff fully trained for their role?

    - What further training in appraisal interviewing and other appraisal-related techniques may be required?
    - When was the last time an audit of appraisal training needs was carried out?

      • With what result?
      • Should it be carried out again now?
      • Who should conduct it?

Assessment of potential

22. Is the individual's potential assessed as an additional part of the procedure? If so, how is potential assessed?

    - On past performance?
    - Personality factors?
    - A combination of the two?
    - Or what?

23. Are the particular problems associated with this aspect of assessment recognized? By all concerned? Are you sure?

    - Is potential considered in a subjective long-term way involving a broad prediction of latent talent? Of ultimate job level? Or is it specific in terms of shorter-term promotability (e.g. 'now', 'in one year', etc.)?

24. Are the assessments of potential valid? How do you know? What evidence is there that past assessments have been accurate?

    - For instance, are all those individuals rated as having high potential, or being immediately promotable (say) three years ago, still with the organization? Is the organization helping them positively to realize their potential? What are these people doing now? If a marked proportion has since left, what does this imply about the quality of this aspect of development practices in your organization?

25. Who makes the assessment of potential?

    - The individual's immediate manager?
    - The senior manager?
    - Personnel/training staff?
    - A combination of the above people?
    - Someone else?
    - Are they competent to make such an assessment?

        • Are you sure?
        • Again, what evidence is there currently to show that the assessments made are valid?

26. Is the individual concerned informed of what his or her potential/promotability is considered to be?

    - What is your justification for this approach?
    - Is it fair to the individual?

27. Are meetings an effective way to discuss an individual's potential/promotability? Have alternative, perhaps more objective, ways of doing so been considered?

    – For instance, what use does your organization make of assessment centres in assessing potential?
    – Could their use be introduced or extended?

Follow-up

28. What happens to the completed appraisal forms?

    – Who keeps them? For how long? Are they regarded as working documents? Or are they merely additional paperwork to be filed?
    – If each appraising manager does not have at least a summary of the results, why not? How can action be taken subsequently?

29. Is there an internal appeals procedure for those not happy with their assessment?

    – Does it work?
    – How often is it used? What does your answer suggest about the programme's worth?
    – If no appeals procedure is operated, what should be done? When? By whom?

30. Is effective action taken on the recommendations made in individuals' appraisals? How do you know?

    – What control mechanisms exist to ensure that the recommendations are actioned as appropriate? Do these mechanisms work? Are you sure?

31. Are individual development needs fulfilled using a wide variety of approaches and not merely off-the-job training courses?

    – Do supervisors and managers recognize that on-the-job development invariably makes a much more significant contribution to success?

32. Which of the following on-the-job development activities play a positive role *now* across departments in your organization?

    – Coaching and guidance?
    – Job rotation/secondment?
    – Special assignments/working party membership/projects?
    – Planned delegation?

How do you know?

33. What other possible development activities not mentioned here could be introduced?

34. What benefits are built into the system for the manager who is both conscientious and effective in appraising his or her staff? Are they sufficient? Against what criteria?

Overall evaluation

35. If one aim of your organization's system is to identify training needs, does it do so?

   – What training needs (both current and developmental) have been fulfilled directly as a result of identification through the appraisal system in the past year? Are you happy with the answer?
   – Is the system really fulfilling this aim?
   – What specific responsibility do individual supervisors and managers carry for taking action on the training needs of their own departments?

   • Are they proactive in meeting these needs?
   • Do they take the initiative or wait to be prodded by the training department?
   • Or do they abdicate altogether?

   – Do supervisors and managers recognize that one of their prime tasks is to help their people develop?
   – How effective are your organization's supervisors and managers in this respect? Is that effective enough?
   – What action does your answer indicate?

36. If another aim is to provide for management succession by promoting internally rather than appointing externally wherever possible, is this aim met?

   – Does your organization operate an effective search/placement system (i.e. 'in-house' recruitment/selection?)
   – If so, do the appraisal results form an integral part of the system?
   – Is the system operated willingly by line management?

   • If indispensability is used as a reason why a particular individual cannot be released for promotion elsewhere in the organization, is a time limit (say three months) imposed? If not, how many people may be languishing because they are too good to let go?

- Does the system work?
  - What is the current ratio between internal and external appointments? Has this ratio risen/fallen/remained static over the past five years?
  - What action, if any, does your answer indicate?

37. What (other) aims does your organization's system have? Should similar questions be asked in relation to these aims?

    - On efficiency? Are things done right?
    - On effectiveness? Are the right things done?
    - On contribution to corporate plans?
    - On acceptability?

    In broad terms are these aims met?

38. In the light of your answers to these questions, does it appear that your organization is operating effectively in this area? Or is there a shortfall between what happens and what you consider to be the best practice?

39. Could part of the problem lie in the resources devoted to the function?

    - Are they merely adequate? Or even inadequate?
    - In either case what could be done to
      - Resource the function more effectively?
      - Encourage a more proactive approach on the part of all concerned?

40. What else could be done to ensure that every member of staff makes an optimum contribution to corporate success?

22 Performance appraisal: Preparing for the interview

Managers tend not to prepare adequately for the appraisal interviews in which they are involved. For many staff it is the only formal occasion in the year when they can discuss matters which concern them. Evidence suggests, however, that such discussions do not have the positive effect on job satisfaction which might reasonably be expected.

Reflecting before the event on what you can do to achieve more fully the aims of the appraisal interviews you conduct will help both you and your staff to derive greater job satisfaction.

Background considerations

1. What are the stated aims or purposes of appraisal in your organization?

2. To what extent do you 'massage' the formal aims towards what you think they ought to be? If your answer is 'not at all', are you sure?

3. Do you accept that periodic review of the performance of your staff with them is an integral part of your job as a manager?

4. Are you fully committed to the process of appraisal? If not, what are you saying about your own chances of progression in the organization? And about treating your staff fairly in this respect?

5. Are you fully competent to discharge your commitment?

    – How many days' training have you undergone in relation to appraisal processes?

    – How long ago did the most recent training take place?

    – When was the last time you read an article or a book on the subject?

    – What action, if any, do your answers suggest?

6. Are you absolutely sure you appreciate why the appraisal is to be conducted?

Preparing for the appraisal

7. What information do you have by which you will judge the individual's performance?

    – Is it really sufficient from your point of view?

    – Is it enough from the individual's point of view?

    – Assuming that a self-review is an integral part of the procedure, have you studied the individual's response in detail?

    – If a self-review is not carried out, why not? Is the individual sufficiently involved? Is review something done genuinely with people, or merely about them?

    – Could you request a written self-review in this case?

    – Are you now in a position to make an objective assessment? Are you sure?

8. What actions were agreed with the individual for this appraisal period? What priorities were agreed?

9. Which parts of the job were particularly testing? In what ways?

    – Time needed?

    – Time available?

    – Personal application?

    – Ability?

    – Interpersonal skills?

    – Or what?

Why? Was it planned? What is the individual's view?

10. How far was the individual's performance affected by circumstances? Did these circumstances help or hinder performance? How? To what extent?

11. What is your overall view of the individual's performance?

    – How well has the individual performed against each target?

     – How closely does your view compare with that of the individual?
     – Was more achieved than you expected? Or less? Why?
     – Which tasks were performed particularly effectively? Less effectively? Why?

12. What particular abilities has the individual displayed in performing the tasks? How could these be developed further?

     – What action could the individual take personally?
     – What joint action/commitment could be agreed?
     – What personal commitment from you may be appropriate?

13. What particular lack of ability may have prevented the individual from achieving success? As a result, what specific action could be taken to ensure success in the future?

     – By the individual?
     – By you?
     – By both of you jointly?

14. What, if anything, is the individual doing in relation to his or her own self-development?

     – On whose initiative?
     – What does your answer indicate about the individual's approach to the job?
     – What part should your answer play, if any, in the written appraisal? In the subsequent discussion?

15. What scope is there to develop the job? To what extent has the individual done so? How far does it seem the individual might do so in the future?

     – What action, if any, do your answers indicate? On the individual's part? On your part?

16. How often have job-related progress discussions taken place during this appraisal period? With what effect? Have the discussions been reflected in extended performance? What reference should be made to this aspect in the written appraisal?

17. Having considered the background to the appraisal in broad terms, are you now in a position to complete your detailed analysis of the individual's performance during the appraisal period? Do you recognize that the quality of your analysis will affect directly the quality of the subsequent discussion with the individual?

18. What possible tasks and priorities for the next appraisal period should be covered during the interview?

19. How should the interview be structured? What do you want to include? What may the individual want to discuss? What should the agenda be? Are you clear in your own mind what has to be covered? And in what order?

20. At what point will you inform the individual of the place, date and time of the interview?
    – Will you ensure that the individual has sufficient time to prepare?
    – Is the timing favourable? For both of you? Are you sure?
    – How will you make certain that the discussion is conducted in private and that there will be no interruptions?

21. Are you sure you will allow sufficient time in your diary for the interview?
    – Have you allowed a contingency period within the time (say half-an-hour) to ensure that the interview is not interrupted?

22. If you have allowed less than $1\frac{1}{2}$ hours in total for the interview, are you sure you are giving both of you the best chance to succeed?

23 Performance appraisal: Conducting the interview

The appraisal interview is often viewed with dislike by both parties. It can, however, be a powerful means of promoting mutual understanding, furthering staff development and enhancing job satisfaction. This checklist leads you through the steps needed to make your appraisal interviews successful and useful for yourself, your staff, and the organization.

Planning

Preparation

1. Have you prepared an interview plan by studying all the necessary information about the individual and his/her record over the review period? (See Checklist 22)

2. Have you notified the individual concerned so that he/she can also prepare for the interview?

Privacy

3. Will the interview be held in private to ensure that you will not be disturbed?

Nil interruptions

4. Do you accept that there should be no interruptions in an interview of this type?

Time

5. Have you allowed enough time for the interview?

 - Have you made every effort:

 - To hold the interview when the circumstances are favourable?
 - To avoid a time when the individual is likely to be on the defensive (for example, just after you have drawn attention to some mistake he/she has made)?

The interview

Creating the atmosphere

6. Is the interviewee put at ease from the beginning?

 - Do you accept that he/she may be anxious and that a few casual remarks may help to create a friendly atmosphere?

The purpose

7. Do you:

 - Explain the purpose of the interview (that it is performance oriented and that you expect a two-way exchange of information)?
 - Emphasize that you are there not to criticize but to help?

The discussion

8. Is the individual asked how he/she views his/her job performance and the results achieved?

 - Is this approach used to pave the way for the remainder of the interview?

Praise

9. Do you:

 - Make a point of mentioning work which has been done well?
 - Offer congratulations on accomplishments?
 - Use the good points of the assessment to give praise wherever it is justified?

Criticism

10. Do you:

   – Accept that people usually know when they have fallen short in some respects and are often willing in a discussion to indicate their deficiencies themselves?
   – Ask questions tactfully to assist the individual to appreciate any weaknesses if there is a reluctance to discuss shortcomings?
   – Guide the discussion, if necessary, to any significant area(s) of weakness?
   – Encourage the individual to suggest ways of overcoming these weaknesses?
   – Make sure you do not avoid 'bad' points?
   – Have the proper evidence to support critical comments?
   – Make blunt comments only if the situation demands it?
   – Ensure that any criticism is constructive?
   – Avoid using words which could result in a defensive reaction?
   – Accept that using words like 'faults', 'weakness', 'failure', 'bad', 'inadequate', often have this result?
   – Adopt a positive approach, such as 'You could improve . . . by . . .'?
   – Share responsibility when things go wrong, for example 'We can do better if we . . .'?

Conclusion

11. Do you:

   – Make a note of anything you have said you will do to help?
   – End the interview on a positive forward-looking note?

12. Does the individual know:

   – What improvements are expected?
   – What assistance and guidance can be expected from you to help achieve the improvements?

Summary

13. In brief, when analysing job performance, do you:

   – Encourage the individual to say how he/she views his/her performance and the results achieved?
   – Direct questions towards the individual's strengths and, in particular, his/her weaknesses?
   – In the last resort, draw attention to the weaknesses?

   – Ensure that comments are supported with adequate evidence?

14. When considering ways of improving, do you:
    – Ask for suggestions or remedies in the first instance?
    – Draw attention to possible remedies and improvements?
    – If these are not forthcoming, tell the individual what improvements you expect?

After the interview

15. Did you:
    – Make the purpose of the interview clear?
    – Follow the plan for the interview?
    – Give the individual time to think out his/her answers to questions?
    – Listen to the replies and not just hear them?
    – Review adequately both strengths and weaknesses? What areas of weakness were discussed? What were the individual's reactions?
    – Obtain suggestions from him/her about what personal action could be taken to improve performance?
    – Gain commitment from him/her on the action he/she has promised to take? How will this be checked?
    – Consider what other help would be needed?
    – Promise to investigate any queries he/she may have had?
    – Clarify and agree the individual's tasks and priorities for the period before the next interview?
    – Make a note of agreed action?

16. What are your own self-improvement plans to improve future appraisal interviews?

24   Personal planning

There is much wisdom in the old saying, 'If you don't know where you're going, how will you know when you arrive?' Planning permits a measure of control over your time and your life, and brings benefits at home as well as at work. It is useful from time to time to consider how much effective, implemented planning you are doing, and how much the events of your daily life are controlling you.

1. To what extent do you plan your life? At work? At home? Elsewhere? Or does your life have a tendency to plan you?

2. Reviewing your efforts over the past twelve months, how many of your previous plans were actioned successfully? And an end-result achieved? At work? At home? Elsewhere?

    – What main results were achieved?
    – What proportion of your plans did these successes represent?
    – To what extent were you successful without having to work for it? How much happened by coincidence? By 'lucky breaks'?
    – How far did any lack of success result from 'bad luck'? From 'unlucky breaks'?
    – What other successes/failures did you experience in the same period?

        • Were the successes planned for?
        • Were the failures the result of ineffective planning? If so, how specifically? Were the failures caused by a lack of, or even 'bad', luck?
        • To what extent may you be depending on luck rather than judgement in your own personal planning?

Focus of plan(s)	Date agreed/ formulated	Interim objective(s) (if appropriate)	Final objective	To be achieved by (date)
Your job – maintenance – development				
Your domestic life – relationship – other commitments				
Your life elsewhere – relationships – other commitments				
Your personal development – professional skills – professional knowledge base – reduction of negative traits (e.g. procrastination) – balance of learning styles – learning to learn				
Your leisure time – protection – extension – other				
Your health – fitness – stress control – other				

Indicate priority: *xxx* Must; *xx* Should; *x* Could

Figure 24.1 Plans in progress

3. What do your responses to these questions suggest about the calibre of your personal planning?

   – How far is your success planned positively?
   – How far is any failure the consequence of poor planning?

4. To what extent could the quality of your thought processes in respect of planning the 'what' and 'how' of your life be influencing the outcome? Do you invariably plan for success? Or does your lack of planing tend to produce the opposite effect?

   – How many crises seem to happen to you in an average week?
   – How often could people be thinking of you in terms of the old adage: 'Your lack of planning yesterday, does not constitute a crisis for me today'?
   – To what degree do you believe it would be possible to improve your approach to planning the various elements of your life?

5. Do you want to 'free up' your thinking about planning issues?

   – If so, are you prepared to be honest with yourself?
   – If not, do you recognize the likely impact on:
     • Your professional reputation?
     • Your domestic reputation?
     • Your reputation elsewhere?

6. If you decide to unblock your thinking further in this respect, complete the table shown in Figure 24.1.

7. Reviewing each of the areas in which you have indicated that plans have been formulated, to what extent does each plan meet the criteria illustrated in Figure 24.2?

   – Are you satisfied with your answers? Or does the reverse apply?
   – Which of your plans do not specify success criteria (end-results)?
   – Which 'plans' are nothing more than vague intentions?
   – What are your priorities currently? Are they sufficiently balanced between the environments in which you operate?
   – Which of your 'plans-in-progress' require further development and clarification? What should be done? How soon? And involve who else, if at all?
   – Which are the areas in Figure 24.1 where you have indicated that you have no plans to do anything at present?
     • What are the reasons for your lack of plans?
     • Do these reasons bear close scrutiny?
     • Would it be worth thinking through your responses again?

8. Looking again at your personal list of 'plans-in-progress', are you now comfortable with them as they are written? If not, can you reduce the degree of discomfort by reviewing your plans further?

   – Having completed the review, are you now committed to each one of your 'plans-in-progress'?

9. Are your plans now feasible? Suitable? Acceptable? Within whatever cost, time or other constraints which apply? Do they allow for contingencies (any effects of Murphy's Law)? Incorporate suitable control and monitoring mechanisms? And specify clear end-results?

10. What other plans may be appropriate in view of your responses to this checklist? In terms of the constituent elements of well-drafted plans? Of balancing your plans to include all the major areas of your life? Of keeping a close check on the progress of your plans to fruition?

    – Whatever additional plans are appropriate, will they also be tested against the criteria illustrated in Figure 24.1?

11. To what are you now committing yourself with all your plans? Will you use your responses to engage positively in your own personal development over the coming months?

    – How long will it be before many of your current plans are relocated 'on the backburner'?
    – How much will you continue to procrastinate in any area of your life?
    – Should the underlying causes of any likely procrastination be addressed directly?
    – When?

Capability	Does the objective suggest that you are over-reaching yourself? Is it realistic? Is it practical? An accurate reflection of the need? Representative of the pursuit of excellence, rather than perfection? Using resources which are available, or which can be made available? Within current capabilities? Achievable with effort? How risky is the objective? Is the degree of risk acceptable? How will you cope if things go wrong?
Clarity	What results do you want to achieve? Are the 'success indicators' clearly stated? Is the objective expressed in quantitative terms? – Quantity: How much? – Quality: How well? – Cost: At what cost? Is there a clear indication of when any interim objective(s) must be achieved before the primary objective is achievable? Is the relationship between priorities and time-frames clearly stated? Is there a clear time-window? Are the 'musts' and 'wants' clearly identified?
Coherence	Is the objective phrased in such a way that you will know when you have reached it? Is it expressed as a totally unambiguous statement of intent?
Consistency	Is the objective consistent with your broad role? Is it within your own sphere of responsibility? If you are stepping outside your role, are you quite clear why? Is the objective consistent with your domestic responsibilities? Your responsibilities elsewhere?
Compatibility	If there is more than one objective, is each compatible with the remainder? Will the achievement of one objective detract from any other?
Cancellation/ curtailment	What sort(s) of emergency would result in your plans being 'put on hold'? Or cancelled completely? What would be the cost to you personally?
Commitment	Having reviewed the parameters of the objective, are you committed to its achievement? How far into the future are you committing yourself?

Figure 24.2   Planning criteria

25   Personnel profiles

There are a number of well-known methods of specifying the ideal candidate for a particular vacancy. Perhaps the most commonly used is the one originally put forward by Professor Alec Rodger and known as the 'Seven point plan'. The headings used here, and the supporting questions, are based on this method.

A personnel profile (or person specification) can be derived from the job description and a knowledge of the physical and social conditions in which the job is performed. Not all the headings are necessarily relevant for every profile: it is wiser to concentrate on a smaller number of critical attributes.

The personnel profile performs an important role in the selection process: its use as a yardstick against which candidates are assessed should not be underestimated.

What are the attributes required in a successful candidate for a vacancy?

First impressions

1   What sort of first impression should the successful candidate give? In terms of appearance? Dress? Cleanliness? Voice? Manner? Social experience? Poise?

Knowledge, skills and experience

2   What does the job require in terms of:
   - General education and examinations passed? How important is fluency in languages or other specific academic attainments?
   - Specific training (e.g. trade apprenticeship, national certificate, specific courses on knowledge/skill areas)?

  – Relevant experience (e.g. type of work, length and level of responsibility)?

Mental ability

3. How 'bright' should the successful candidate be in relation to the population as a whole? What level of analytical ability is appropriate?

Aptitudes

4. How far does the job require particular facility in:

   – Understanding mechanical principles?
   – Working with computers?
   – Drawing aptitude?
   – Verbal expression?
   – Manipulating tools, components, etc?
   – Musical or artistic talent?

Leisure interests and activities

5. How far does the job require skill in:

   – The social sphere? (Persuading, managing, understanding, helping, entertaining or being with people?)
   – The practical–constructive sphere? (Manipulating, repairing or constructing things?)
   – The physical active sphere? (Outdoor pursuits or those involving considerable physical effort and agility?)
   – The intellectual sphere? (Solving problems requiring a scientific or logical approach?)
   – Artistic expression? (In colour, design, layout?)

Personal qualities

6. What does the job involve in terms of:

   – Initiative?
   – Reliability or steadiness?
   – Loyalty?
   – Acceptability to others?
   – Conformity to existing attitudes/behaviour in the department/ organization?
   – Decisiveness?

- Influencing others or taking the lead among them?
- Self-reliance?
- Acceptance of responsibility?
- Emotional maturity?
- Perseverance?
- Readiness to learn?

General background

7. Is it advisable that the successful candidate should be without dependants? Able to travel?

    - Is personal financial stability important?
    - Is a fidelity bond appropriate?

Motivation and expectations

8. What levels of expectation will the job satisfy with regard to:

    - Pay/salary and fringe benefits?
    - Recognition?
    - Achievement?
    - Application of professional knowledge?
    - Career progression?

How hard will he/she have to push himself/herself? How much energy/effort is appropriate?

Health

9. What standards of general health and fitness are required? Are there any particular points which are important concerning height, strength, special strain on limbs, vision, hearing, handedness, ability to work under particular job conditions?

10. Have all the above attributes required in the successful candidates been considered? Have priorities been realistically established? Has a distinction been made between essential attributes (musts) and desirable attributes (wants)? Has any possible over-prescription of essential attributes been avoided? Are you sure?

11. What measurement criteria will be used, particularly for intelligence and personality? Is a medical examination part of the selection procedure? If so, is the doctor aware of the requirements indicated in the profile? Is he/she sent a copy before the examination takes place?

12. Are there any contra-indications? (Any negative attributes which would mean immediate disqualification from further consideration, for example a candidate under a driving ban applying for a job as a travelling sales representative.)

Personnel Profile

.... (Job title)

Factor	Attributes	
	Essential	Desirable
1. First impressions		
2. Knowledge, skills and experience		
3. Mental ability		
4. Aptitudes		
5. Leisure interests and activities		
6. Personal qualities		
7. General background		
8. Motivation and expectations		
9. Health		

Contra-indications (if any) ....

....

....

If applicable, minimum test results acceptable:

Intelligence
Personality
Aptitude
Other (specify)

Prepared by .... Date ....

Job description no. ....

Figure 25.1   Example of a personnel profile

26   Preparing a presentation

Persuading a group of people is no easy task. It can be made even harder by lack of preparation. To be accepted, your proposition must not only be good, it must be seen to be good. And this requires detailed planning of what you want to achieve and how it can best be achieved with your particular audience. Taking time to plan and prepare provides an extra injection of confidence when you face the sea of faces, and smooths the way for your powers of persuasion to work.

Your intentions

1. What is your general aim in giving this particular presentation? To inform? To persuade? Or what?

    – Can your aim be justified?

2. What are your specific objectives?

    – Are you clear about what you intend to achieve?
    – How long do you estimate you will have to achieve your objectives?

3. Having clarified your answers to the two previous questions, can you now write down your aim? And your specific objectives?

    – Are both aim and objectives expressed in active terms?
    – Can they be achieved in the time available?

4. Now reflect on what you have written. Do your aim/objectives require further modification? Are they really achievable within the time you will have?

Your audience

5. How many people will listen to your presentation?

6. Who are they?
    - What do they know already?
    - What are their particular interests? Attitudes? Prejudices?
    - To what kind of approach will they respond best?
    - What will be your 'selling proposition'?

7. Do your aim/objectives need further revision as a result of your answers?

Preparation

8. What do you know already about the background to your proposed presentation?

9. How can you find out more?
    - Conversation?
    - Interviews?
    - Books, magazines, newspapers?

10. Have you perhaps been too enthusiastic? Do you now have too much detail? Or still not enough? What action does your answer suggest?

11. Are you now in a position to prepare an outline of your presentation?
    - Does your outline have a logical framework?
      - Is it understandable?
      - Is it too vague?
      - Could it be shortened and still make sense?
    - How particularly will you gain the attention of your audience?
    - What will they expect? What is the benefit to them?
    - How will they be helped to visualize what you are saying, to 'see' your words?

12. Does your supporting material suffer from the inclusion of any of the following weaknesses:
    - Loose statements?
    - Sweeping generalizations?
    - Imprecise words?
    - Jargon?

- Loose logic?
- 'Padding'?
- Loaded or emotive words?
- False comparisons?

Will this supporting material be genuinely relevant? And understandable? And 'tight' (closely argued)?

13. What visual aids could assist your presentation? Diagrams? Models? Charts? Transparencies? (See Figure 26.1.)

    - Will your aids be kept simple? And suitable for the size of your audience?
    - Will the aids be big enough to see?

    (Remember: For a group of twenty people to read the writing on a transparency the letters should be at least 1.5cm high: never make transparencies from pages of typing – they will ruin your presentation.)

14. Having reviewed your proposed presentation are you sure that:

    - You will be saying what you mean?
    - Meaning what you say?
    - And adopting a balanced approach?

15. Would a written summary of your presentation be appropriate as an *aide mémoire* for your audience afterwards? If so:

    - Will it be concise?
    - Will it have visual impact?
    - Will it be fully supportive of the presentation itself?

Practice

16. Will you practise your presentation before the event?

    - Is it worth listening to it on a tape recorder beforehand?
    - Do you know your opening sentences by heart? And your closing sentences?
    - Have you prepared appropriate cue-cards?

17. Is your presentation now part of you? Are you ready to give it?

Which of the following aids, or combination of aids, would add visual impact to your presentation?

The item itself
Do you accept that this is the only visual aid, if appropriate, which can give the correct idea of size, weight, texture and shape?

Model of the item
If use of the item itself is impractical, would a model (if necessary cut away or transparent) be advantageous?

Flannel or magnetic board
Have you considered that these aids are particularly useful if you want to move material around on the board during the presentation?

Chalk board/whiteboard
Whilst this may be useful for a limited presentation, do you remember that the writing must be large enough for everyone to see? And clear? And that spelling errors can negate its usefulness?

Electronic whiteboard
How useful could this be to offer photocopies of your 'work' on the board to participants?

Flip chart
Bearing in mind the points relating to the use of chalk or whiteboards, might a flip chart be useful if the same material is required for more than one presentation?

Films/videos
If you intend to use a film/video, will you make sure you preview it first yourself? Will it add to your presentation or be your presentation? Will you be using the film/video for the right reason? Have you ensured that there will be an effective introduction (including a statement of why the film/video is being used)?

- Will a technician operate the projector/video player? Will you? If so, are you familiar with its operation?
- Are you sure you know what to do if something goes wrong? Have you planned for the subsequent discussion? How?
- Have answers been prepared for likely questions?

Figure 26.1   A selection of visual aids

Slide projector
Do you recognize that the main advantage of using a slide projector rather than a film is the control which you can exercise over the speed, content and sequence of the presentation? And that this advantage is minimized by using a video player?

Overhead projector
Have you considered that an overhead projector has all the advantages of chalk/flannel boards? And most of the advantages of flip charts? Are you also aware of the added advantages that:

– It does not prevent you facing your audience throughout the presentation?
– The transparencies are easily stored and portable?
– You can easily switch the audience's gaze from the screen to you (and vice versa) in order to emphasize particular points?

If you do use transparencies, will they be prepared professionally? Or will you prepare them?

– Will the number of *words* illustrated be severely limited? And big enough to see? And legible?
– Will the words be combined with symbols and pictures?
– Will the final transparencies positively support your presentation? And definitely not *be* your presentation?

Video recording/playback
Have you considered the usefulness of this aid for product training, re-runs of role-playing exercises and the like?

Have you considered the use of all these aids in the context of the timing of your presentation? How far in the future is it? Will this affect the availability of films, videos, preparation of transparencies or other material?
How often will similar presentations be given in the future?
How often will other presentations be given where the use of particular aids would add impact?
Which of the visual aids indicated above does your organization possess now?
Would it be worth investing in one of the more costly aids?

Figure 26.1   concluded

27 Preparing for negotiation

Successful negotiation depends on detailed planning. Researching the topic, preparing the case thoroughly, accommodating likely contingencies, knowing your own strengths and relative weaknesses (and those of others involved) are all part of the process.

Applying mature personal judgement during the negotiation itself, based on previous planning, will help to ensure a successful conclusion.

Introduction

1. Do you accept that negotiation takes place whenever you are involved in a situation where the intention is to change relationships?

2. As a manager, do you recognize that you spend a considerable proportion of your time negotiating?

3. Have you ever undertaken a formal training course in negotiation? Or have you learned purely by experience?

4. If so, has the experience been cumulative? Do you consider yourself to be a successful negotiator?

5. Is there room for improvement? If so, have you ever analysed your basic approach to negotiation?

6. Are you aware that there are two basic types of negotiations – integrative (mutual interest) and distributive (I win – you lose)?

Mutual interest negotiations

7. Do you accept that:

    – The aim of this type of negotiation is to make certain that everybody gains something?
    – This aim can only be achieved by agreement?
    – Agreement itself can only result from recognition of mutual interests?
    – Mutual interests can never be recognized if you are pressing for the best possible deal? A lesser percentage of a good thing is better than 100 per cent of nothing?

'I win – you lose' negotiations

8. Do you accept that:

    – This is a conflict bargaining approach?
    – It is concerned with the allocation of limited resources?
    – Your aim is to negotiate the best possible settlement from your own point of view?

General negotiating considerations

9. Are you aware of the differences implicit in these two types of negotiating?

    – That if either the required settlement, or the likely problems encountered in reaching it, are fundamentally different for each side, then the negotiation is likely to be of the 'I win – you lose' type rather than the 'mutual interest' type?

10. Do you also recognize that:

    – Both types may be encountered in the same negotiation, but that your strategy and tactics will depend primarily on your recognition of which type predominates?
    – Your opponents's perception of the situation and the strategy/tactics he/she uses are equally important?

Self-knowledge

11. Do you know yourself?

    – Have you ever assessed yourself? What action is indicated on your part?

– What are your strengths as a negotiator? Your weaknesses? What improvement action are you taking? For instance, do you know when to stop? To forgo an advantage? Can you 'wait in haste' when there may well be a temptation to act impetuously or give in to provocation?

Knowledge of opponent

12. Are you aware of your opponent's strengths and weaknesses? Motives? Needs?

13. What does he/she want from the negotiation? Personally? For others?

Listening technique

14. Do you accept that a good negotiator is able to maintain a balance between intelligent listening and effective speaking?

15. Do you recognize that listening is as much a persuasive technique as speaking?

16. Are you a good listener? When listening do you:
    – Think ahead and anticipate reactions?
    – Weigh the evidence?
    – Think about what has been omitted and decide whether it is relevant to the negotiation?
    – Recognize the different levels at which your opponent's statements can be considered?

      • What he/she *seems* to be trying to communicate.
      • What can be inferred from the way he/she communicates and the words used.
      • What he/she conveys by the manner of approach to the subject.

    – Make every effort to observe and interpret the details of your opponent's non-verbal signals (gestures, facial expressions, movement of limbs, blinking, coughing, yawning, etc.) which can reveal emotional state?

Preparation

17. Having considered these background issues, how do you feel your preparation could be improved? Would fuller consideration of the following issues be helpful?

18. *Aims*

    – Who has instigated the forthcoming negotiation? You or someone else? Or is the negotiation periodic?

      • If you: What is your specific aim in entering this negotiation?
      • If someone else: What is his/her specific aim, if known (if not, the most probable aim)?
      • If periodic: What is the joint aim? What precedents have already been set?
      • Is it an 'I win – you lose' or 'mutual interest' situation?
      • If agreement is to be based on mutual interest, what is the widest possible divergence mutually acceptable?
      • What will be the *minimum* negotiated position acceptable to you? What points will it also be preferable to achieve?

19. *Research*

    – Do you have all the necessary background information? Have you done the necessary research?

      Facts/figures
      • What do you know already?
      • What do you need to know?
      • What would you also like to know?
      • What is your opponent's position on the above questions?

      Those involved
      • Have you recognized all the interested parties to the negotiation?
      • Do you know your opponent(s)? Their strengths? Weaknesses?
      • Who would like to maintain the 'status quo'?
      • What do they really want from the negotiation?

20. *Indicated action*

    – Based on the above, what action, if any, can you take now to strengthen your position for the negotiation? How?
    – Can you use the grapevine to transmit and receive information? Or informal meetings?
    – Can you condition your opponent's reactions/expectations?
    – Can you change the timing of the negotiation, by either bringing it forward or putting it back, to better suit your own aim(s)?
    – What action, if any, might you be able to force your opponent to take to strengthen your position?

21. *Indicated restraint*

   -   Is there anything you can stop doing to strengthen your position?
   -   What, if anything, can you stop your opponent doing which will strengthen your position?

22. *'Rules'*

   -   What 'rules' are applicable?

      •   What existing agreements must be upheld?
      •   Has a time limit been placed on the negotiation? By whom?
      •   Alternatively, is there a natural time limit?
      •   Does the time limit favour you? Or your opponent?
      •   Are there any penalties involved in the negotiation (such as a penalty for bluffing or giving false information)?
      •   Can many items be introduced into the negotiation simultaneously?
      •   What would be the cost of a stalemate?

23. *Assumptions*

   -   What assumptions have you made about the negotiation? Do you recognize them?
   -   Do you accept that assumptions when taken as absolute fact can be a serious obstacle to successful negotiation? That you are taking a calculated risk if you do accept assumptions as fact?
   -   Have you calculated the risk?
   -   Will these assumptions be tested during the negotiation?
   -   What other 'hidden' assumptions may be made?
   -   What assumptions is it probable/possible that your opponent has made?

      •   How will this affect your thinking?
      •   Are there any 'assumed' certainties?

24. *Contingencies*

   -   Have you allowed for contingencies, particularly those which may originate from your opposition?

25. *Constraints*

   -   Have you evaluated the main constraints to your case? Your opponent's case?
   -   How will this affect your assessment of possible alternative approaches?
   -   Have you considered the tactical possibilities bearing in mind:

- Your aim?
- The strength of your negotiating position?
- Your opponent's strength?

26. *Tactics*

   – Will your tactics be offensive or defensive? Punch or counterpunch?
   – Have you considered the various tactical approaches open to you?

   Your opponent's case
   - Will you let your opponent make his/her case first?
   - Are you ready to question his/her facts? Assumptions? Conclusions? Any omissions/inconsistencies in the case?
   - Are you ready to amplify any weakness and use it to consolidate your own position?
   - How will you amplify such a weakness?

   Your opponent
   - If your opponent maximizes the strengths (and minimizes the weaknesses) of his/her case, are you prepared to adopt the maxim 'If you can't beat the case, beat the person'?
   - If so, have you considered deprecating his/her experience, etc? Or even exceeding your opponent's physical/mental exhaustion threshold?
   - Have you examined his/her personal weaknesses?
   - Are you sure you can cope?

   Your own case
   - Will you go for the 'second shot'?
   - How will you best indicate the benefits of your case to your opponent?
   - Will you maximize the strengths of your own case whilst also maximizing the weakness of his/hers?
   - Are you ready to demonstrate mastery of the details of your case?

Readiness

27. What else have you learned from previous negotiations which will help you to be more effective this time? Are you really ready for the negotiation?

28   Problem solving

Dealing with day-to-day problems skilfully is the basis of effective decision making. Such skill is not developed overnight. It is the product of much experience and trial and error. The approach taken here is based firmly on logic and illustrates a step-by-step method for analysing, and dealing with, the work problems you encounter.

Defining the problem

1.   What is the nature of the problem?

    –   What is the extent of the problem?

        • What is going wrong?
        • Does it concern one limited area or does it impinge on other areas?
        • Is it generating conflict within these areas or between management in these areas?
        • What more could go wrong if nothing is done?

    –   What is its significance?

        • Are there any social, political, environmental, legal or religious aspects?
        • How does the problem affect other people?
        • How does it relate to the corporate culture?

    –   Is it an isolated problem or is it associated with a cluster of existing or latent problems?

        • Does the problem relate to a 'once-for-all' issue, or is it likely to recur?

- • Could its solution provide political leverage for dealing with other problems?
- • What additional opportunities might be 'opened up'?

– Can you locate the problem on the quadrant illustrated in Figure 28.1?
– What quadrant description appears to be most appropriate: simple/static (easiest to deal with), complex/dynamic (the hardest) or what? Remember: you have most time to deal with a quadrant 1 problem, and the least time to deal with one located in quadrant 4.
– What would be the cost of doing nothing?

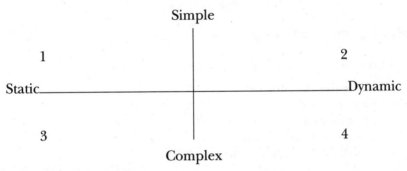

Figure 28.1   Problem location

2. What is your aim in solving the problem?

   – Can your aim be stated precisely?

      • What do you want to achieve ultimately?
      • Have you set for yourself an intended state of affairs – a target?

3. Do you recognize that the gap between the present state of affairs and the target is a problem-gap to be bridged?

   – Can you identify the various factors which constitute the obstacles to a solution? Are these factors controllable or uncontrollable? How predictable or unpredictable are they as future factors?
   – What are the chief flaws, weaknesses or deficiencies which must be put right?
   – Have you listed these critical factors (the problem dimensions)?
   – Can you rank them in order of importance?
   – Can you also 'weight' these factors? Assume for instance that you have 100 points to allocate between them. (This approach – listing, ranking and then weighting the critical factors – is helpful in establishing which are the toughest issues you must deal with first and the sequence in which you should tackle them.)

4. Can you now:

   – Restate your aim?

     • Is it realistic? Practical? Achievable?
     • Is it measurable?

   – Clarify the criteria which must be met by a solution? (Cost, time, percentage changes, ratios, degree of risk etc.)
   – Identify the problems to be overcome? In priority? Can you identify clearly your 'musts' in relation to 'wants'? (Perfection vs excellence, efficiency vs effectiveness.) Does the aim truly answer the question 'How will I know when I've got there?'

Analysing the problem

5. Who must:

   – Make the decision?
   – Be consulted?
   – Be informed?
   – Discuss the problem?
   – Translate the decision into action?

6. Have you resisted all the 'common-sense' exhortations to find out the facts first?

7. Do you remember that no one knows which facts are relevant until the problem has been defined and classified? And that until then all data are just 'raw data'?

8. Have you considered what information you need?

   – How relevant, representative, reliable and valid are the data you have now?
   – What additional data do you need? In what form?
   – Have you reviewed all the possible sources of information open to you?

     • People? Their knowledge? Their experience? (Networking)
     • Places?
     • Documents?
     • Own knowledge?
     • Own experience?

9. Have you examined and re-examined your pool of information?

   – Does it reveal that you have wrongly identified the problem or wrongly classified it?

10. Have you taken into account that:

    - Not all facts will be available?
    - Some will be too costly to obtain?
    - There may not be enough time?
    - Any search for additional information may represent only a marginal gain?
    - Compared with 'need to know' information, the 'nice to know' equivalent can prove expensive to generate? If so, have you noted and acknowledged your guesses and assumptions? Have you accommodated the constraints on your analysis?

Generating options

11. Do you accept that developing a range of options is difficult because everyone runs the danger of seeing only one pattern – the one they are accustomed to?

12. How can you generate options?

    - By reviewing other cases to search for an analogy?
    - By brainstorming the problem – suspending judgement to allow the free flow of ideas?
    - By other methods? If so, what?

Evaluating options

13. Have you generated sufficient choice? What are the relationships between the options, if any? Are they mutually exclusive? Or can they be recombined?

14. Has each option been considered in turn against:

    - The criteria set (cost, time frame, etc.)?
    - Degree of risk?

        • Have the risks been weighed against expected gains?
        • What are the associated opportunities and threats?

    - Commitment over time?

        • For how long would the organization be committed by the decision? Would the decision constitute a precedent? With what implications?
        • How quickly could the decision be reversed? Could it *be* reversed?

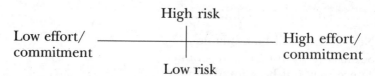

Figure 28.2   Risk/effort identification

- **Economy of effort?**

    • Which of the possible courses of action will produce the greatest results with the least effort? Are you mindful that the greatest results may require the greatest effort?
    Do not choose the easiest option too soon: it may not be the 'best'. For instance, how far does the degree of effort/commitment compare with the degree of risk, as shown in Figure 28.2?
    • What other similar comparisons may be appropriate?
    • Which option will produce the needed change with the least disturbance to the organization?

- Legal imperatives?

    • What legal requirements must be considered? National codes of practice? Industry codes of practice? (Have internal procedures also been considered?)
    • How might they be invoked? With what effect? At what cost?

- Timing?

    • If the problem is urgent, would a dramatic approach be best? What would be the likely repercussions of such an approach?
    • Should it be kept secret? Could such secrecy be justified? Are you sure?
    • If it is a long-term course of action (Figure 28.1, quadrant 1?), would a slow, steady start be advisable?

- Resources?

    • Are the necessary resources available to carry out the plan? If not, what time-scale would be necessary to make them available?
    • What would be the effect on, and of, the people involved? Their particular personalities? Attitudes? Skills? Knowledge?
    • Could any vested section/department interest sabotage the plan?

Remember: it is no use solving one problem to create another. What could be the 'knock-on' effect? What new, and different, problems could be generated?

15.   Can you now decide on the 'best' (your preferred) option?

Preferred option

16. Have you decided:

   - What action must be taken?
   - Within what time frame it will be actioned?
   - By whom?
   - Who will implement the decision?
   - When they should be informed?
   - How they should be informed?
   - Who else should be told?
   - How they should be told? (See Checklist 16.)
   - What contingency plans are necessary?

17. Have you written down the details of the plan systematically so that all concerned will know:

   - The background information to the problem?
   - The aim of the plan?
   - The operational method?
   - The administrative support?
   - The communication network?

     • Who should be informed for action? For information purposes only?

   What else could/should you do to ensure the fullest understanding/ commitment?

18. Have you established a control and monitoring system?

   - What checks will be needed? For how long?
   - Have the contingency plans been fully accommodated?
   - What progress reports will be needed? From whom? To whom? When?

   Are you ready now to put the plan into action?

Review

19. Has the solution been effective? Fully? To what extent was it necessary to reconcile variances? To implement your contingency plans? For what reasons?

20. What lessons have been learned for the future? By you? By others? What action does your answer suggest?

   Decisions often have to be made quickly, and frequently the satisfactory one must be accepted in place of the ideal. These questions provide a 'hard' strategy – a stimulus to thought in the analysis of problems and in decision making from one particular perspective. They do not represent a sequence which must be slavishly worked through every time a problem arises, as shown in Figure 28.3.

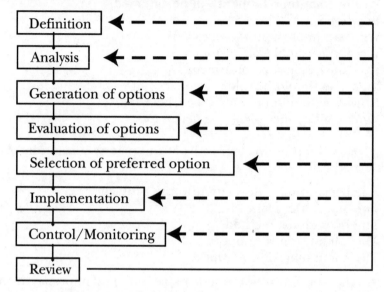

Figure 28.3   Problem solution: some pathways

Is it worth considering an alternative ('soft') strategy? If the distinction lacks meaning for you, what action may be appropriate? When?

29 Procrastination

Procrastination is a familiar part of life: so often it *seems* easier to put tasks off, to let things drift, rather than take action. Yet at the same time we may be aware that our procrastination is having an adverse effect on us, and possibly on our relationships at work and at home. Recognizing the extent of the problem and clarifying the reasons for our inaction will clear the way for greater proactivity – and eventual elimination of the problem.

1. To what extent do you believe that you are an efficient manager of your own time? An effective manager of your own time? And even an excellent manager in this respect?

   - Do you do things right?
   - Do you do the right things?
   - And do you do the right things right as far as managing your time is concerned? How do you know?

2. What evidence can you produce which supports your responses? Is it 'hard' evidence? Or merely opinion?

3. Reflecting on your own personal 'outstanding tasks' list, how many arose more than a week ago? At work? At home? Elsewhere?

4. What proportion of your 'outstanding tasks' list have you tackled in the last seven days? At work? At home? Elsewhere?

   - How many of the 'top-priority' ('must do') tasks have been completed?
   - How many remain? In all three environments? If not, in which, particularly?
   - To what extent have you been tackling those tasks which you prefer to be involved in rather than your priority items?

5. What are your responses to these last two questions (3 and 4) when set against other time-frames?

    –   What tasks have arisen over the past fortnight? How many have you completed? How many remain?
    –   How different is your list now compared with four weeks ago? Twelve weeks ago? Six months ago?
    –   How many tasks remain on your 'outstanding tasks' list which arose more than six months ago? At work? At home? Elsewhere?
    –   What is the proportion of 'must do' tasks to 'should do' tasks? And to the 'could do' tasks?

6. What do your answers to all the previous questions tell you about your willingness to procrastinate?

    –   To what extent do you tend to put off, for any reason, tasks which you know must be done?

- It will go away if I ignore it.
- It is not my job. I won't do anything until I know it really is mine.
- I shall be criticized.
- I do not have the resources/information, and so on.
- It is very important . . . far too big a job to start now. I do not have the time at the moment, or the energy, or the space, to get started.
- I am a perfectionist – if I think long enough I am bound to find a better way. That is why I am not tackling it now.
- It really does not matter – it is not important.
- I shall probably make a mess of it when I do get round to tackling it.
- I shall upset people . . . or they will upset me . . . probably both.
- I am not in the mood.
- I would rather do something else which I find more stimulating/pleasant/rewarding.
- I prefer working under pressure . . . I will wait until the problem/task reaches critical mass, then I will do it.
- What is the point? Whatever I do will only get changed by the boss. I will have wasted my effort.

Figure 29.1   Some possible 'justifications' for ignoring tasks or potential problems

- Are you generally slow to complete outstanding tasks? Or are there particular examples about which you have a blockage, and which therefore do not get done? How important are these tasks in your own personal scheme of things?

7. Whatever your responses, might it be that you are detracting unnecessarily from your professional reputation by putting things off? And also detracting from domestic relationships? And relationships elsewhere?

- Could your procrastination be preventing you from being a truly efficient, and an effective (even excellent) time-manager? In all three environments? Or one, particularly? If so, which?

8. If you do want to reduce, and even eliminate, your 'procrastination quotient', are you prepared to be honest with yourself?

9. If so, what are the reasons you use to yourself, and possibly to others, to justify your procrastination? Which of the 'justifications' shown in Figure 29.1 seem to apply particularly to you?

10. Would it be worth checking your perceptions of your preferred justifications for inaction with the perceptions of other people close to you?

- Is the relationship between you and your colleagues at the same level in the organization sufficiently firm for the issue to be discussed with them? With your boss?
- What about your domestic situation? Would it be worth seeking the views of your partner?
- Or is any discussion totally out of the question for you? If so, can you confront the reasons which underpin your decision for continuing confidentiality? What does your answer say about you?

11. In either event (discussion with others; private introspection), what seem to be the main ways in which you 'put off' tasks?

- Or is it unsafe to generalize?
- Is your approach at work different from that which you use at home? Or elsewhere?
- What are the implications of your response?

12. Whatever the ways in which you personally procrastinate, and the environment(s) in which you do so most, how far does your experience of life and people suggest that you have been successful so far in doing so? Or does the opposite apply?

13. If so, what may have been the impact of your procrastination on your professional reputation in the past? What do you think the impact might be now?

'Excuse' Implication	Tick (✔) as appropriate		
	Definitely an excuse I use	Definitely not an excuse I use	Need to change my approach in this respect
1. **'It will go away'** Will it? Are you sure? Or is it more likely that you will have to deal with it sooner or later when it becomes urgent?	☐	☐	☐
2. **'It is not important'** Is this just an excuse, or is it truly unimportant? If so, cross it off your list.	☐	☐	☐
3. **'It is not my job'** Are you sure? Or only half-sure? You must find out one way or the other, otherwise you may be in for a nasty shock.	☐	☐	☐
4. **'I'll probably make a mess of it', 'I'll be criticized', 'I'll upset people'** Why? Is it because you do not have sufficient information? Or feel that you don't have the necessary skills? Is your attitude to the task/problem realistic? Are you seeking perfection?	☐	☐	☐
5. **'It is too big/important to start now'** If it really is big/important it will have to be attacked sometime. And big jobs are only collections of smaller jobs with a different label. Why not try to isolate the smaller jobs and tackle them first? (You eat the biggest meal one mouthful at a time!)	☐	☐	☐

6. **'I'm not in the mood'**
    Fair enough for the moment.
    But when will you be in the
    mood? Is this a one-off situation?
    Or do you use your mood as an
    habitual excuse?

7. **'I'd rather do something else'**
    How clear are your 'must/
    should/could' priorities?
    Should they not be dictating
    what gets done when?

8. **'I'll leave it until the last possible
    moment'**
    If the task is completed within
    the specified time-scale, fine up
    to a point. But what happens if
    rush jobs arise? Or if there are
    other contingencies? How wise is
    it to leave any task until the last
    possible moment?

9. **'There is bound to be a better
    way'**
    There probably is, but are you
    searching for perfection?
    Wouldn't the pursuit of
    excellence be more realistic?
    And practical? You can overplan
    unnecessarily and use this as an
    excuse for avoiding action.

10. **'It will only be changed anyway'**
    If this is a task for which you are
    responsible, you will have to do
    it sometime. Why not discuss the
    merits of any changes with the
    person who wants to make
    them? You may learn something
    valuable for next time.

Figure 29.2   The implications of your procrastination: an assessment

14. How has putting off tasks affected your chances of promotion?

15. What could be the impact on your career if you continue to procrastinate at the same level as you have in the past? As you do now? And what could be the effect on your domestic life?

16. Can you justify any further procrastination about reducing the type and number of tasks you 'put off'? Are you sure?

17. Is the problem:
    - Deciding what action to take?
    - Or deciding to take action?
    - And when to take it?
    - All three?
    - Or identifying the causes of the blockages which encourage you to procrastinate?

18. Are you prepared to do something positive about your past procrastination? Now? Today?
    - Are you prepared to be more proactive in planning your life? Or will you continue to allow your life to plan you?

19. If you are committed to taking action, are you prepared to re-examine the excuses you use for putting things off? Do these excuses stand up to close scrutiny?

20. What are your reactions to Figure 29.2?

21. Now review your current list of 'outstanding tasks', and against each item note a realistic time-frame for successful completion.
    - What are the implications of ignoring each item on your list?
    - What would be the likely impact on your job performance? On harmony at home? And elsewhere?
    - What would happen if you did nothing?
      • What could be the repercussions?
      • For you personally?
      • For the organization you represent?
      • For relationships?

22. By the same token, what would happen if you did complete each of the items on your list?
    - Would your job performance be enhanced?

- Would your job satisfaction be enhanced?
- Would your feeling of general well-being be enhanced?
- Would relationships be consolidated?

23. Looking back over the last two questions (21 and 22) which seems to be the more positive route for you? Action? Or reaction?

24. To what extent are you now committing yourself to act positively in minimizing, and even eliminating, your tendency to 'put off' any tasks which need to be completed?

25. On which aspects of the topics included within the checklists in this book have you decided that action on your part is necessary?

    - How long is it since you made the decision on particular issues? (See Figure 29.3.)

26. What does your analysis of Figure 29.3 suggest should be done? When? In what order? Using what control documents? Could the form shown in Figure 29.4 play a part in helping you to minimize/eradicate your propensity to put things off?

Topic (checklist)	Action decided .... months ago							Degree of procrastination to date			
	1	2	3	4	5	6	7	None	Low	Mod.	High
1.											
2.											
3.											
4.											
5.											
6.											
7.											
8.											
9.											

Figure 29.3   Proposed action

Topic (checklist)	Action decided .... months ago							Degree of procrastination to date			
	1	2	3	4	5	6	7	None	Low	Mod.	High
10.											
11.											
12.											
13.											
14.											
15.											
16.											
17.											
18.											
19.											
20.											
21.											
22.											
23.											
24.											
25.											
26.											
27.											
28.											
29.											
30.											
31.											
32.											
33.											
34.											
35.											
36.											
37.											
38.											
39.											
40.											

Figure 29.3   concluded

27. How committed do you feel at this moment to the *mañana* philosophy of 'never do today what you can put off until tomorrow or, preferably, the next day'?

28. How proactive do you intend to be, starting now, about eradicating the negative effects of your inaction at work? At home? Elsewhere?

   – Are you prepared to respond by identifying/analysing/evaluating the elements of your procrastination – and then by taking positive action?

TO DO
THIS DAY/THIS WEEK/THIS MONTH/THIS QUARTER/THIS YEAR
(Highlight/circle as appropriate)

1.

2.

3.

4.

5.

6.

7.

8.

9.

10.

Signature . . . .   Date. . . ./. . . ./. . . .

Figure 29.4   Outstanding tasks (To do) form

30 Recruitment

The costs to an organization of recruitment can be high. But the costs of poor recruitment are dramatically higher. Recruitment-created disasters such as the wrong people for the job, lack of suitable candidates for interview, shortfall of labour and many other familiar problems have a direct impact on the organization. A formal policy document for recruitment can provide valuable guidance to prevent these disasters, but it must be up to date, especially in the light of current employment legislation.

Recruitment policy

1. Does your organization have a formal recruitment policy?

    –   Do all those concerned, both directly and indirectly, have copies of the policy statement? If not, why not?
    –   When was the last time the policy was updated?
    –   Why was it updated then? Should it have been updated since?
    –   Does the current statement include reference to the following objectives?

        •   To promote the PR image of the organization?
        •   To attract suitable candidates for individual vacancies?
        •   To motivate these people to apply?
        •   To eliminate unsuitable replies?
        •   To achieve the above cost-effectively?

    –   If not, what action is indicated? By whom?

The vacancy

2. Why has the vacancy arisen?

    – Does it have to be filled at all?

        • What would be the consequences of not filling it?

    – Could the work be distributed among existing staff?
    – Have the possibilities of using technology been fully explored?
    – Could the work be subcontracted?

Background information

3. Has a job analysis of the position been carried out? Has a job description been prepared? Has a specification of the ideal person (a personnel profile) been derived from the job description?

Time-scale/numbers required

4. Over what time-scale will candidates be required?

    – Is the requirement immediate or ongoing?
    – If it is ongoing, for how long?

5. How many vacancies are there?

    – How many people will need to be considered to fill these vacancies?

6. What effect will the answers to these questions have on the decision to use a particular recruitment medium, or combination of media?

Sources of recruitment

7. Do you consider internal candidates first? If not, why not?

    – Is the job standard too high?
    – On what grounds is external recruitment justified?
    – Has the balance been weighed between 'new blood' and the knowledge of the business and its environment possessed by existing employees?

8. Is a 'potential employee' register kept of recently unsuccessful applications? Do you use it?

9. If you have to recruit externally, what recruitment services do you use now? Which of the following are used:

   – Job Centres?
   – Local Authority Careers Service?
   – Recruitment agencies?
   – Schools/Colleges/Universities?
   – Professional institutes?
   – Trade unions?
   – Consultants (including 'headhunters')?
   – Introductions by existing staff?
   – Personal contact?
   – Cinema?
   – Television?
   – Direct mail?
   – Recruiting units:

     • Mobile?
     • Shop premises?

   – Newsagents' windows?
   – Display units?
   – Notice boards?
   – Newspapers:

     • National?
     • Regional?
     • Local?

   – Trade/professional/specialist press?
   – Broadsheets (freesheets)?

10. Is the use of these media based on the answers to the following questions?

    – What level of candidates is required (unskilled, skilled, clerical, professional, managerial, other)?
    – How many are required?
    – When will they be required? By what time? Over what time-scale?
    – At what cost?

11. Are you aware of how much the use of these media is costing your organization? Individually? In total? Over what time-scale?

12. Are you getting value for money? How do you know?

13. What efforts are you making to locate new, more cost-effective sources of candidates?

Recruitment records

14. Do you keep the following recruitment records?

    - Number of candidates replying through specific media (including newspaper advertisements)?
    - Number of candidates called for interview for a particular vacancy?
    - Number of interviews for each vacancy?

15. Are these records acted on continuously? If not, why not? When was the last time the effectiveness of the recruitment records system was reviewed?

Management responsibility

16. Who is responsible for recruitment? How long has he/she had this responsibility? Are all the implications of this responsibility understood? How do you know?

    - Is the responsibility effectively carried out? By what criteria?
    - Is initial/follow-up/booster training required? On what, specifically? When?

Preparation of advertising copy

17. Who is responsible for preparing advertising copy?

18. Are the following factors considered to be important when preparing advertising copy?

    - Qualifications?
    - Place of work?
    - Duties/definition of responsibility?
    - Starting salary/salary range?
    - Required experience?
    - Details of the organization?
    - Prospects for advancement?

19. Are you aware that these factors are important to potential candidates?

    - In fact do you ensure that the advertising copy takes full account of candidates' point of view?
        - Is the heading/job title itself meaningful?
        - Is the copy interesting?

- Will it persuade suitable people to reply?
- Is it made easy for them to reply?
- Do you remember *not* to ask for photographs or specify a closing date?
- Are the implications of using a box number fully appreciated?

20. Is the organization's name considered sufficient to 'sell' a vacancy? How good is the organization's reputation as an employer? Can it be improved? How?

21. Do you accept that a recruitment advertisement, if well prepared, is a good advertisement for the organization in the broadest sense?

Cost of recruitment

22. What was your organization's recruitment budget in the last financial year?

   - Was it overspent or underspent? Why?
   - Whose responsibility was it to check spending?
   - Was the amount spent cost-effective?
   - What was the per capita cost of recruitment?
   - What proportions of the amount spent were devoted to particular media? Does the 80–20 rule apply?
   - Can the procedure as a whole be made more cost-effective?

31 Report writing

The ability to prepare a well-structured concise written report which achieves its purpose is not as widespread in organizations as might be supposed, although it can be developed relatively easily. A systematic approach, understandable to the reader, is the foundation of a good report, and can be achieved with practice.

Background considerations

1. Why are you writing this particular report?

   - Is the report really necessary?
   - Are you sure?

2. What are your objectives in writing the report?

   - Have you defined these objectives clearly?
   - Do the objectives state unambiguously what you intend to achieve?

3. Is the report your own idea? Or someone else's?

   - In either event who will read it?
   - To whom should the report be sent on completion? For action? For information?
   - Who are you really writing the report for? Why does that person matter most?

4. How will the report be used? Bearing in mind your answer to the previous question, what information should be presented graphically? Diagramatically? Pictorially?

   - How can you ensure maximum impact on the reader?

5. When should the report be presented?

   - When is the report needed?
   - Will you allow a contingency period within your planning to accommodate any results of 'Murphy's law'?
   - What would be the consequences of late presentation? For the organization? For you?

6. How should the report be presented?

   - Under a covering memo?
   - In person?
   - In some other way? How?

The report

Title
7. What is the title?

   - Does it reflect accurately the contents of the report? Are you sure?
   - What expectations might the title create in the reader?

Contents
8. Is there a table of contents?

Summary
9. Is there a summary? Is it clear and concise?

   - Does it contain a clear statement of your objectives? Your conclusions? And your recommendations?
   - Is it no longer than one A4 page?

Introduction
10. Does the introduction provide a frame of reference for the reader? Has it defined the background to the report? The current situation? The theme of your report? The method you have adopted for analysis?

    - Does it act as a reminder?

Headings
11. Is the text grouped under main headings?

    - Is each main heading of approximately equal importance?
    - Are the headings presented in a logical progression?
    - Do they exclude each other?
    - When considered together, do they equal the subject of the report?

Words used

12. How will the reader react to the words you have used in the report?

     –   Have simple words been used? Or are they complex?
     –   Are they concrete? Or abstract?
     –   Have unnecessary words been included?
     –   Will the reader be able to picture the meaning readily?
     –   Have active verbs been used?
     –   Have clichés and stock phrases been used too frequently?
     –   Do any specialized terms require explanation? Would the inclusion of a glossary of such terms be useful?

Sentences

13. Do sentences average not more than about 20 words? And say what you mean without any ambiguities?

14. Are sentences varied in length? And suitably punctuated to help the reader understand?

Paragraphs

15. Do paragraphs have topic sentences?

16. Is each paragraph limited to a single topic? And limited in length?

17. Do the paragraphs progress naturally?

Conclusions

18. Are your conclusions drawn exclusively from the main text of the report? Are you sure?

19. Have you made any inferences which are not fully supported in the text? Have you checked?

     –   Are the facts of the case clearly distinguishable from your opinions?

Recommendations

20. Are your recommendations based firmly on the conclusions? Are you sure?

21. Are the recommendations realistic? Practical? Legal?

     –   Are they fully costed?
     –   Are time frames clearly specified?
     –   Do they relate directly to the objectives defined at the outset?
     –   Are they presented in order of priority?
     –   Are any constraints on action clearly identified?

Appendices
22. Have you numbered any appendices?

23. Are the appendices referred to in the main text? Is there any unnecessary detail in the main text which would be more effectively presented as an appendix?

Distribution
24. Has the distribution list been clearly indicated?

   – Who should not see the report?
   – What would be the consequences of sight by any unauthorized person?
   – What actions, if any, do your answers suggest?

25. Is there a clear definition of who is expected to take action as distinct from those who are receiving the report for information purposes only?

Presentation
26. Does the front of the report indicate clearly who originated it? And when?

   – Is the title of the report suitably emphasized? For example, has it been 'boxed' and featured prominently on the front page?

Quality assessment

27. In money terms, how much has it cost in total to prepare the report?

   – Your time?
   – Others' time?
   – Use of equipment?
   – Materials?

28. Was the money well spent?

29. Are you pleased with the physical presentation of the report?

   – Is the print clear?
   – Is the paper suitable?
   – Are the covers appropriate?
   – Do the pages turn easily?
   – Is the report easy to handle?
   – Will it stand usage?

30. Are you pleased with reactions to the report? Has the action taken

subsequently on your recommendations justified the cost of producing the report? Are you sure?

- If not, what does your answer say about the quality of the report? Or its need?

31. What actions, if any, do your answers to the four previous questions suggest?

32. What actions do your answers to *all* the previous questions suggest? Could it be said of any report you prepare that you write to express? Or impress? . . . How do you know?

32 Salary policy and administration

Few things can damage the industrial relations climate of an organization so swiftly as a sense of injustice over salaries. Salary policy needs to be fair – and seen to be fair. This applies not only to starting salary but also to pay increases and bonuses. If salary policy is based on job evaluation, the basis for the evaluation needs to be understood and agreed as fair by the workforce before the salaries which result will be accepted. And the link between performance appraisal and salary increases also needs to be clear.

1. Does your organization have a salary policy?

   – Is it written down?
   – Who was responsible for formulating the policy?
   – Was it the result of consultation prior to publication?
   – If it is not written down and a copy made available to all employees, why not?

2. Who is responsible for administration of the salary policy? Is it the Personnel function? Financial function? Or some other function? Is that the right function? If not, what should be done to change the situation?

3. Is the salary policy based on job evaluation? Are all jobs in the organization included in the evaluation? Is the evaluation itself based on job descriptions? If not, why not?

4. What method of evaluation is used?

   – Ranking?
   – Classification?
   – Points rating?
   – Factor comparison?

162

- Or a combination of two or more of these methods?
- Or some other method?

5. Who is responsible for job evaluation in your organization? Is the responsibility accepted and understood? Are there periodic reviews? What are the periods of review?

6. Does the organization have a job evaluation committee? Who are the members?
   - Are they the right people?
   - Are union/staff association members included?
   - Is there an appeals procedure?
   - How often is the appeals procedure used?
   - Does this reflect on the job evaluation method used?
   - Or on its application by the people concerned?

7. Is there a formal salary structure (with established minima/maxima for different grades/ranges of jobs)? If not, why not?

8. Is everyone made aware of the grade/range to which their particular job belongs? How? Do they have to ask or are they informed?

9. How competitive are your organization's salaries?
   - Are checks periodically carried out to ensure that rates are competitive in the locality?
     - Regionally?
     - Nationally?

10. How are these checks made?
    - Through employment agencies?
    - Contact with other companies?
    - Job vacancies advertisements?
    - Consultants?
    - Or how?

11. Who makes the checks? Are they acted on? When was the last time such a check was made?

12. How are salary reviews made? On an *ad hoc* basis? Through performance appraisal?

13. If it is not through performance appraisal, can the situation be justified? How?

- Has it ever had to be justified?
- What was the result?
- What action was taken?
- Should any further action be contemplated now?

14. When are salaries reviewed? Annually? If so, when? Does it follow the performance appraisal? How closely?

15. How long does it take for the performance appraisal results to be actioned through salary adjustments? If more than a month, why?

16. Is a clear distinction drawn between cost of living increases and merit increases?

    - Is 'cost of living' regularly reviewed? How?

      - Through the retail price index?
      - Or some other method?
      - Is this the right method?

    - Who carries out the review?
    - Who is responsible for action?
    - Is that the right person?

17. Does any cost of living adjustment take place at the same time as salary adjustments? If so, is a clear distinction made between them? If not, why not?

18. Are cost of living adjustments applicable to all staff at the same time? If not, what problems may this cause between different groups of employees?

33   Selection: The interview

There are three stages to an effective selection interview and they each require equal weight in the mind of the interviewer. They are: preparation; the interview itself; and the post-interview phase. An unprepared interview will probably be a disaster. The interviewer will obtain little useful information and the interviewee will be given a poor impression of the organization. Proper preparation ensures that the interviewer's objectives are clear, and greatly enhances the chances of success. After the interview, there are a number of issues to be considered, for which the last section of this checklist will prove a helpful aid.

Checklist 12 contains some useful questions on interviewing in general.

Preparation

1. Are the preparations complete? Do you recognize that such preparation is a prerequisite of a successful interview?

2. Has the job been analysed and a job description been prepared? If not, how can you possibly know what is expected of the successful candidate?

3. Has the personnel profile been prepared?

4. Is it an accurate reflection of the job description?

5. Do you now have a clear idea of the sort of person you are looking for?

6. Have you studied the application form in detail and prepared an interview plan?

7. Does the interview plan include critical questions and areas requiring

clarification/confirmation which have arisen from your study of the application form?

8. Do you have answers ready for likely questions by the interviewee on the job itself, for example conditions of service, salary progression, sickness benefits, pension?

9. Has initial reception been arranged (gate/receptionist informed)?

10. Are facilities in the waiting room acceptable?

    – Temperature?
    – Company literature?
    – Comfortable seating?
    – Toilet facilities?

11. Are facilities in the interview room acceptable?

    – Temperature?
    – Appropriate seating?
    – Nil interruptions?
    – Calls taken by switchboard/secretary?

12. Have you stated a specific time for the interview? Has the interviewee confirmed his/her acceptance?

The interview

13. Is the interview effective? Do you remember the following basic advice?

    – Stick to the time stated?
    – Allow the interviewee time to settle down?
    – Make notes, but remember to ask the interviewee's permission first?
    – Establish a pattern of questioning that the interviewee can follow?
    – Probe vague replies?
    – Ask open-ended questions (for example, 'Tell me about . . . ')?
    – Observe the interviewee's reactions?
    – Listen 'between the lines'?
    – Get facts which will enable you to make a positive decision?
    – Give the interviewee a chance to ask questions?
    – End by explaining what will happen next (for example 'We will be in touch with you by Wednesday week')?

    Do you remember *not* to:

    – Grill the interviewee by asking difficult questions at the start?

- Allow the interviewee's answers to your favourite questions to assume disproportionate importance?
- Talk yourself for more than a quarter of the time?
- Make assumptions about the interviewee?
- Ignore gaps or inconsistencies in career pattern?
- Ask multiple questions?
- Ask trick, ambiguous or leading questions?
- Allow small items to colour your judgement?
- Criticize or show disapproval of the interviewee?
- Make moral judgements of the interviewee?
- Regard the interview as a platform for your own knowledge and opinions?
- Tell the interviewee your decision during the interview?
- Indicate possible acceptance (for example, 'After you join us')?

Post-interview procedure

14. Is the post-interview procedure effective?

Making the choice

15. After each interview for a vacancy:

   - Have you allowed time for reflection, note-making, any other action, before the next interview?

16. After all interviews for a vacancy have been completed:

   - Have the facts about each applicant been compared with the requirements laid down in the personnel profile?
   - Have references been checked?
   - If a medical examination is part of the process, is the result satisfactory?
   - Is a final rank order of acceptability then drawn up?
   - Do you base your decision on all the facts available?

17. Once the decision is made do you ensure that all concerned are informed speedily of the outcome?

   - Is the offer to the successful candidate confirmed in writing?

18. Do you allow for the possibility that your first choice may reject the offer? As a result, are the rejection letters held over pending acceptance?

19. Once acceptance is confirmed and a starting date agreed have you ensured that:

     – All necessary joining information is sent (including where to report and to whom, on the first day)?
     – National Insurance Card, Income Tax Form (P45) are requested for handover on the first day?
     – Help is offered to solve problems connected with:

        • a move into the locality (for example, home purchase)?
        • transport difficulties?

     – All concerned with the new employee's induction into the organization are aware of their responsibilities?

General considerations

20. Are interviewee's expenses covered?

21. Do you have standard (not duplicate) letters of acceptance and rejection? If not, might it be worth considering their introduction as a time saver, particularly if you deal with a large volume of candidates?

     – Do you recognize that even a rejection letter, if phrased in the right way, can enhance your organization's image?

22. Do you keep to the date by which you confirmed you would contact each candidate after interview?

     – Do you recognize that failure to do so can adversely affect the organization's image?

23. Do you keep the following selection records?

     – Number of vacancies filled internally?
     – Number of offers made?
     – Number accepted?
     – Number started work?
     – Cost per head per new starter?

24. Do you check the progress of new appointments to assess the validity of your selection judgement?

     – What is the proportion who prove unsatisfactory in follow-up?
     – Is it steady/rising/falling/nil?
     – How do you control the cost-effectiveness of the procedure?
     – Are labour turnover statistics checked regularly?
     – Do they validate the recruitment/selection procedure?

   –   If not, what can you do to rectify the situation?
   –   Do you learn from your mistakes?

25. Would it be worth while considering other selection methods?

34   Selection: The process

The human resource of an organization is a costly one, when all the on-going costs of employment are taken into consideration and multiplied by the number of years that these costs will be incurred. So selection of these human resources needs to be as effective – and cost-effective – as possible. Many organizations still rely on old-fashioned and statistically invalid methods of selection, with managers who pride themselves on being able to 'pick the right ones' at interview! Familiarity with the wide range of modern selection techniques is more likely to generate cost-effective selection and reduce the costs of turnover and mismatches.

1. To what extent do you believe that your organization is both efficient (things are done right) and effective (the right things are done) in:

    – Selecting candidates for employment?
    – Promoting internal candidates to more senior positions?

2. What data particularly have informed your response on the quality of your organization's selection processes?

    – How many external candidates were appointed to positions within your organization during the last complete financial year? And how many have been appointed since?
    – What is the proportion of appointments to the number of candidates considered? To the number of candidates invited for face-to-face meetings?
    – How many, if any, of these external appointments were made without being subject to a competitive selection process?
    – To what extent does an 'old pals' network operate in your organization? How many appointments do you believe are being made using this network?

   – What was the total cost of recruiting/selecting all external candidates to appointments within your organization:

      • In the last financial year?
      • And since then?

   – What is the average per capita cost of recruitment/selection currently?

      • Is this cost rising in absolute terms? Steady? Falling?

3.   How many of these externally-appointed candidates, however they were chosen, are still employed within the organization?

   – What is the percentage rate of retention currently for all those appointed since the beginning of the last complete financial year?
   – Conversely, what is the crude rate of staff turnover?
   – How does the rate compare with that which applied:

      • In the previous financial year?
      • And the year before that?
      • Is the figure rising? Steady? Falling?

   – How many have been promoted since appointment? What is the percentage rate of promotion from the pool?

4.   How many internal candidates were promoted (from within the organization) to new positions in the last complete financial year? And since then?

   – What proportion of these internal promotions were subject to a competitive internal selection process?
   – What proportion were appointed without the vacancies being advertised through the organization's internal communication channels?
   – How many such appointments do you know of?
   – How many more might there be?

5.   How do these figures for the last complete financial year, and since (in terms of external appointments, subsequent promotions, and internal promotions), compare with the average number of people employed in your organization in the same periods? How do the figures compare with the ethnic grouping(s) of staff within your organization? With the numbers in each age-band? With their gender?

   – Has selection and promotion been balanced? Or the opposite? What might be the explanation?
   – Is your organization complying with current equal opportunities legislation?

- In the spirit as well as the letter?
- What evidence do you have for your response?
- Are you certain that such evidence is 'hard', rather than being based on opinion?

6. Who makes selection decisions in your organization?

   - Who is involved in appointing people from outside the organization to posts within it?
   - Who is involved in appointing internal candidates to promotion positions?
   - Can you identity those involved? Those who make the decisions?

     - By section?
     - By department?
     - By division?
     - By occupational level?

   - Are the decision makers you have identified the right people to make such decisions in your view?

     - Should others be involved?
     - If so, who?

   - Is the authority and responsibility for making such decisions written into the formal job description/terms of reference of all those involved?
   - If not, what should be done? How soon? By whom? In consultation with who else?

7. Having identified the decision makers in this respect throughout your organization, are they competent, and fully experienced, to perform the task of selecting new staff or promoting existing staff?

   - What evidence do you have which supports your answer?

8. Have all selection decision makers received formal training in selection processes? In interviewing techniques? In non-interview selection techniques? In equal opportunities legislation?

   - If so, how recently? And for how long? On what specifically?
   - Has the impact of this training on selection results been evaluated? How? When? With what result?
   - If selection decision makers have not received formal training, why not?

     - How does your organization cope with the likely results of such lack of training?
     - Is it coping?

- How do you know?

  - If only some selection decision makers have received training, what specifically needs to be done? How soon?
  - What booster training may be necessary for those who have received initial training? What re-training may also be necessary? Re-development?
  - To what extent do 'new appointment' selection decision makers receive training in selection processes before taking up their appointments? And, if not, immediately after appointment? Again, what action is indicated? How soon should it be taken? By whom? In consultation with who else?

9. Has your organization's stance on selection/promotion issues been committed to paper in the form of a policy statement?

   - If so, what reference is made to the commitment:

     - To train comprehensively those who take selection decisions?
     - To fulfil the legal and moral obligations of the organization as an employer?
     - To ensure equity of treatment?
     - To select on the basis of merit alone?
     - To do so on the basis of a full analysis of particular jobs in order to identify the competences involved?

   - Should the policy statement be reviewed to assess its impact on selection activities currently? And on current concerns about, for instance, sexism, racism and 'age-ism'? Who should review the policy? In consultation with who else? When?
   - If there is no policy statement available, how can individual selection decision makers know within what broad framework they should be operating?

10. Reviewing now your responses to all the previous questions, how efficient, and effective, do you believe your organization's selection processes to be? Are these processes capable of improvement?

    - On the basis of cost (including lost opportunity)?
    - On the basis of quality/suitability?
    - On the basis of statute/natural law?

11. If any of your responses to the preceding questions suggest a possible shortfall in approach, what needs to be done?

12. Which of the techniques illustrated in Figure 34.1 form part of the

Techniques	Occupational level(s) at which used
Interview(s)	_____
Psychometric tests	_____
Proficiency tests (work samples)	_____
In-tray (in-basket) exercises	_____
Biodata analysis	_____
Group exercises	_____
Trainability tests	_____
Leaderless group discussions	_____
Personal presentations	_____
Case study analysis	_____
References	_____
Medical tests	_____
Outdoor activities	_____
Any other assessment techniques (please specify)	
_____	_____
_____	_____
_____	

Figure 34.1   Selection techniques used in your organization

selection process in your organization currently? And at which occupational levels are the techniques used?

13. Now reflect on the details you have incorporated into Figure 34.1. What are the implications of your responses?

  - Do interviews provide the sole basis for selection decisions throughout your organization?
  - Or merely the main basis?
  - If so, at what particular occupational level(s) are interviews used?
  - Are the shortcomings of the interview as a selection technique recognized?

- • How is the proven lack of validity and reliability of the interview justified in your organization?
  - • Or is it conveniently ignored?
- – When was the validity and reliability of any other techniques used for selection purposes last checked in your organization? Or has their use still to be checked? What action is indicated? Who should take it? When?

14. What techniques, other than the interview, are used at different levels?

   – Does your organization use any technique(s) not shown in Figure 34.1? If so, which?

   - • When are they used?
   - • Why?
   - • Are the technique(s) valid?
   - • And reliable?
   - • How do you know?

   – Does use of these techniques better inform the subsequent selection decisions? Or not?
   – Or is information not available to support a positive answer, one way or the other?
   – If this is the case, what should be done? When? By whom?

15. What do all your responses to questions 12–14 suggest about the likely quality and longer-term cost-effectiveness of the selection processes used within your organization currently?

16. In view of the sums involved, is the approach to selection decisions taken by your organization of a sufficiently high quality?

   – Is the approach truly cost-effective in terms of retention rates and productivity considerations?
   – Is your organization getting value-for-money from its efforts at present?

17. What action needs to be taken to audit the current efficiency and effectiveness of selection techniques in your organization? And, on the basis of results, to review the advisability of introducing (of even re-introducing) other selection techniques?

35 Selection: The post-interview assessment

Immediately after each selection interview it is advisable to conduct a review of what took place. Notes taken during the interview – with the candidate's permission, of course – will provide a valuable reminder of answers to questions; general performance and match to the job must also be considered. The checklist below provides a basis for the assessment, which can then be used in conjunction with the personnel profile for the job to judge the candidate's suitability.

First impressions

1. What sort of first impression did the candidate give?

    - What did you notice immediately about physical appearance, bearing and manner?
    - Did the interview get off to a quick or slow start?

Education

2. What information do you have on the candidate's educational background?

    - Which school did the candidate attend?
    - What qualifications have been obtained, to date?
    - What level of qualification has been achieved (for example, class of degree)?
    - What qualifications are not possessed which might be expected?
    - In what other subjects, if chosen, might the candidate have been equally successful academically?
    - What signs of inconsistencies are there in the academic record?

176

- What was the content of the college or university course?
- What subjects were specialized in and why?
- What project work, if any, was undertaken?
- What was made of the opportunities offered in project work, and in general in the college or university course?
- What did the candidate like, dislike, find difficult about the college or university course?
- What factors influenced the choice of academic subject, college, career, previous job?

Experience

3. What was the content of the various jobs the candidate has held?

- Are any specialized skills and knowledge offered?
- With what procedures and techniques is the candidate familiar?
- What was liked, disliked, found difficult about the present or previous jobs?
- What technical or academic interests does the candidate have outside work?

Mental ability

4. How much reasoning ability did the candidate demonstrate? How well did he/she express himself/herself? How good was the candidate's grasp of what was said to him/her? How well were any problems or technical questions tackled?

- What strengths in mental ability were revealed?
- What weaknesses in mental ability were revealed?
- What light do any interests shed on the candidate's mental ability?

Personal qualities and interests

5. How much information did you gather about the candidate in this area:

- Part played in school, college, community life?
- Offices held in societies?
- What has the candidate made of opportunities in holding office?
- Interests actively pursued (intellectual, practical, physically active, social, artistic, domestic)?
- Passive interests?

 – What personality traits seem to be revealed by the candidate's interests?
 – In general what evidence is there that the candidate is:

   • Well motivated?
   • Flexible?
   • Dependable?
   • Acceptable to others?
   • Self-reliant?
   • Emotionally mature?

General background

6. Where does the candidate live at present? What does he/she (and partner,
    if relevant) think about moving?

    – How would a move now, or in the future, affect children's schooling?
    – What openings are there for the candidate in later life?
    – What was the candidate's reaction to any travelling involved in the
      job? To other features in the job?

Motivation and career expectations

7. What has been the candidate's career logic?

    – Why does he/she want to leave the present job?
    – What is the candidate looking for in this job?
    – To what extent would this appointment be a move into a new field?
    – In what direction does he/she show ambition?
    – What ideas has the candidate regarding future career?

Health

8. What factors about his/her health are relevant?

36 Self-development

To take personal responsibility for your own development requires a continuing act of will: not only to assess periodically your development needs but also to persevere in dealing purposefully with these needs. Only you can decide what help, if any, you will need in achieving particular aims, and only you can decide whether your personal investment of time and effort in your own growth is paying appropriate dividends.

In any event, it may be worth noting that if you do positively plan your own development, then it is far less likely to plan you. Can you afford to be reactive, rather than proactive, in planning your own future? The following questions are designed to help you respond proactively to the needs you yourself identify.

Preliminary diagnosis

Your beliefs

1. What are the beliefs, the values, by which you lead your life? At work? At home? Elsewhere?

    -   How have you come to hold these beliefs? What is their origin?
    -   Do they mostly reflect your upbringing? Your education? Or particular people? Or some other influence? If so, which?

2. Are your beliefs consistent with one another?

    -   Do any beliefs vary according to the context in which you find yourself?
    -   How strongly do you hold them?

179

– When was the last time you reviewed where you stand now? What action, if any, does your response suggest?

Your job

3. How are your beliefs reflected in the job you do? And in the effort you devote to your job?

– What do your answers suggest about the work you do? And how you do it?
– Are you in the right job?

4. How would you describe your job to someone who doesn't know you?

– What specifically do you do? What is the focus of your work?
– What are your key areas of responsibility?
– Are you currently successful? By what criteria? How do you know?
– How would others describe your approach to your job? Your current success level?
– What action, if any, do your answers suggest?

5. Do you possess written terms of reference for your job (a job description)?

– If so, is the description accurate? Up to date? Focused on ends rather than means?
– If not, how do you know what your job entails? Having reflected on your answers are you happy with them?

6. What were the results of your most recent appraisal?

– What is your own immediate manager's view of your job performance?
– What development actions, if any, were agreed during the discussion? Who took the initiative in identifying any necessary actions?
– What do your answers suggest about the quality of the appraisal? And your own contribution to it?

Where are you going from here?

Your personality

7. How would you describe your personality to someone who does not know you?

– What do you believe are your strong points as a person? How do you know?

- What do you believe are your weaker points? Again, how do you know?
- What is there, specifically, about you which contributes positively to your job performance? To relationships at home? And elsewhere?

8. How would your colleagues describe your personality?

   - How closely would such assessments match your own self-view?
   - What, if any, are the critical differences in views?
   - What do these differences in view tell you about yourself?

9. How do you get on with your boss?

   - What is the basis of your assessment?
   - What could you do to extend/consolidate this relationship? What action could you take? What could your boss do? Would it be worth talking through the possibilities?

10. Generally speaking, are you assertive in your relationships with others?

    - Do others see you as assertive, rather than aggressive or submissive?

Your knowledge

11. How would you describe your knowledge of the job you do?

    - Are you fully informed about *all* the facts involved?
    - If not, what specifically do you not know which you should know?

      • How could you inform yourself? How soon?

12. How would you describe your knowledge now about the job you might reasonably expect to be promoted into?

    - How could you better inform yourself? What specific action could you take?

13. What action could you take to extend your knowledge of the organization you represent, its culture, operations, markets, competitors and future plans?

14. What newspaper(s), trade magazines, professional journals and other similar material do you currently read?

    - Is your reading genuinely relevant to the three preceding questions?
    - Would it help to read less of more relevant material? Or to develop further your 'speed-reading' technique?
    - What action does your answer suggest?

15. Of the management/professional books you have read in the past year, which has had the most direct impact?

    – What happened as a result of reading this particular book?
    – If you cannot answer readily, what are you saying about your choice of reading in the last twelve months? Or your willingness to read?

Your skills

16. What professional skills do you currently possess? What additional skills will you need in the future?

    – What are you currently doing to acquire such skills?
    – How are you acquiring them? And how do you rate your progress?

17. How proactive are you as a learner?

    – What is your preferred style of learning?
    – What action is indicated if you are not sure?
    – What action are you currently taking to develop a more balanced learning style? Is this sufficient? Are you sure?

18. To what extent could your interpersonal skills be extended?

    – How far could your physical attending skills be improved when you are listening to what people say?
    – Could your psychological attending skills also be improved? For example, how effective are the questions you ask during conversations and at meetings?
    – How effective are you in persuading others to do what you would like? At work? At home? Elsewhere?
    – To what extent could you extend your skill in coaching staff? Do you truly help them to help themselves?
    – Do the various types of interview you conduct invariably achieve their aims? How sensitive are you to the feelings of those around you? And how 'political' are you? How comfortable are you with your responses?

19. Looking back over the past three months particularly, how well have you used (managed) your time? Have you extracted full advantage from the 2000+ hours involved?

    – What, specifically, have you achieved in this time?
    – How much better use could you make of your time? How could such increased effectiveness be achieved?

20. How do you currently rate your capacity to produce novel responses to day-to-day problems?

    – How creative are you?
    – Could your capacity be extended with effort? How?

21. How effective are you at managing the stress of everyday life?

    – What effort particularly do you take to reduce the impact of stress on your job performance? On your health?
    – What more could you do? What should you do?

22. To what extent do you suffer undue stress when making a presentation?

    – Can you identify the causes? What can you do to improve the situation?

23. What are people's reactions to the reports you prepare? Are the reactions invariably positive?

    – Have you received formal training in report preparation? If so, how long ago did it take place? If not, what can you do yourself to improve your skill?

24. What changes to working practices have you proposed recently at work?

    – Have they been implemented? If not, why? If so, was their implementation achieved successfully?
    – How far did an assessment of your organization's culture contribute to the success of the changes? Or their failure?

A personal SWOT analysis

25. The preceding questions illustrate a few of the issues involved in personal competence at work. In broader terms how would you rate your skill as a manager?

    – Which elements of your managerial role do you feel would repay particular attention? Planning? Implementation? Control? Communication? Motivation? Or something else? In terms of knowledge? Or skills? Or both?

26. Can you now complete a SWOT analysis (see Figure 36.1) of your current position? Remember: a Strength allows you to exploit Opportunities which could otherwise be wasted; a Weakness on the other hand could constitute a Threat, both now and in the future.

Factor	Strength	Weakness	Opportunity	Threat
Knowing yourself				
Having clear aims for the future				
– personal				
– job				
Relationships				
– with boss				
– with colleagues				
– with others				
Knowledge				
– professional				
– organizational				
– industrial				
Skills				
– professional				
– learning				
– interpersonal				
– time management				
– creativity				
– stress management				
– presentation				
– managing change				
– reading				

Figure 36.1   Personal assessment: a SWOT analysis

27. Now reflect on your SWOT assessment. What does it tell you about yourself? About your personality? Your knowledge? Your skills? The job you do?

28. What are your main strengths?

    – How can you use these strengths to make more space for yourself over the coming months?

29. What do you consider to be your main weaknesses, if any?

    – What could you do to reduce the impact of specific weaknesses?
    – How could you best use the space provided by your strengths? And minimize any threats?

Your plans

30. To re-emphasize questions 1 and 2, do you accept that your own personal *development* is your own personal *responsibility*? That if you do not help yourself, others are hardly likely to do so, apart from perhaps asking you to attend the odd course? And that such a request might be made at very infrequent intervals?

31. Do you also accept that whilst your own learning is your personal responsibility, you will probably need help from others to achieve whatever targets you set yourself?

32. Are you now ready to plan, implement and monitor your own learning?

33. Can you complete the skeleton action plan, shown in Figure 36.2, indicating your proposed actions in the short term (say three months)? The medium term (up to one year)? And in the longer term?

    - What particular checklists included within these pages may be helpful in refining your proposals?

Factor	Help needed from (name(s))	Target	Achievement by (date)	Follow-up/ monitoring
Short term				
Medium term				
Longer term				

Figure 36.2 Action plan

34. Now reflect on your proposals. Are they realistic? Are they achievable with effort? And within the time-scales you have specified? Are you sure? Which people are you proposing to involve in your learning? Are they the right people? Would it be worth discussing the establishment of a self-help (co-counselling) group?

   - If this term has little or no meaning for you, would it be worth finding out more?

35. Are you now ready to get started on developing yourself? Will you be proactive in this respect? And keep the impetus going? Or will your proposals be overtaken by seemingly more pressing matters, so encouraging a reactive stance?

36. How often will you refer to the action plan you have prepared? How often will it be replaced by a successor? When are you planning to review all the preceding questions in this checklist? Is that soon enough?

   - Do you accept that your personal development must be continual to be truly effective? And that this takes real effort?

37. What do your answers tell you about yourself? Are you happy with the answer?

37   Setting up a learning event

There are many approaches to adult learning. The following questions represent one particular method and are designed to encourage you to review your own approach to the training and development programmes to which you contribute.

Background considerations

You

1.   Who are you?

2.   What are your characteristics as a person? Your values?

3.   What is your attitude to adult learning and self-development?
    -   What do the words 'learning' and 'development' mean to you?
    -   Do you accept and treat adult learners as individuals, with individual learning needs? Are you sure? Do you accept the full implications of the question?
    -   Do you adopt a 'helping' rather than a 'teaching' stance?
    -   Do you positively discourage adult learners from dependence on you?
    -   Do you positively discourage yourself from believing that you know best what is good for them?
    -   Do you see yourself as a co-learner?
    -   To what extent might there be a gap between what you think your approach to learning is (your 'espoused' view) and what it is in practice (your 'in-use' approach)?

4. What are your own learning/development needs in terms of this particular event?

5. What are you hoping to achieve personally?

6. What are you hoping to help the learners to achieve for themselves?

The learners

7. Who are they?

8. What are their characteristics as people? Their values? How different are they from one another?

9. What are their attitudes to learning and self-development?

    – How do they view the words 'learning' and 'self-development'?
    – How do they prefer to learn?
    – Do they prefer to develop themselves? Or be 'developed'?
    – How might they be helped to develop their individual approaches to learning?

10. What are their learning/development needs?

    – How have these needs been identified?
    – Have the learners themselves been involved in the identification of these needs?
    – If not, how will you/they ensure the success of the event?

11. What do they want to get out of the event?

    – How do you know?
    – Could it change as the event progresses?

The organization

12. What are the organization's values? Its views on what should be achieved?

    – What specifically does the organization want? How will success be measured?
    – What would be the political implications of such 'success' or 'failure'?
    – How does the answer fit with your own personal values?

The psychological contract

13. Do all the stakeholders know where they stand in relation to the event? Do they appreciate what adult learning involves?

14. Has an appropriate psychological contract for the event been achieved?

The learning event

The purpose

15. In view of the above answers, what should be the purpose of the learning event? Who should decide it?

16. Should the purpose be clarified before the event? Or should it be left until the event is under way? Again, who should decide? If not the learners, why not?

17. Are all concerned fully aware of the implications of such an approach?

18. What mix of learning aims (informing/skilling/developing) and levels of learning (memory, understanding, application, transfer) is appropriate to this particular learning event?

    – Is the truism that 'adults learn by doing, not by being told' reflected in the purpose?

19. Is the purpose justifiable? Realistic? Practical? Within the constraints which apply? . . . from everybody's point of view?

20. Will the purpose be 'owned' by the learners? Are you sure?

The design

21. In view of the purpose, what learning design is appropriate?

    – Will the learners themselves be involved in deciding the design? If not, why not?

22. What methods/approaches would be most effective in meeting the purpose?

    – In what mix?
    – If the learners are not involved in this decision, why not? Can the approach be justified? From whose point of view?

23. What is the environment within which the design will be implemented?

    – What abilities are assumed in those participating in the event?
    – Are these assumptions realistic?

24. Is the design creative? Capable of being implemented a number of times? Does it need to be?

Implementation

25. What factors should be considered in implementing the design?

    - What should be your role?
    - What should be the role of the learners?

26. Do you possess the necessary mix of interpersonal skills to implement the design? Do you have the ability to:

    - Ask the right questions to help self-discovery?
    - Listen actively without prejudging what is said?
    - Allow learners to make mistakes and take responsibility for their own learning?
    - Withstand the emotional pressure from those who may wish to be 'taught the right way'?
    - Help learners 'own' their own learning?

27. Have you the necessary conviction to persist in this approach even when feelings are running high? Are you sure you can be 'comfortable' in your persistence?

Evaluation

28. What evaluation of the learning event should there be?

    - Who should make the decision?
    - If the learners themselves are not to be involved, why not?
    - When should the broad decision be taken?

29. What methods should be used?

    - What alternatives are available?
    - Who should review them?
    - How should the different perceptions and needs of those involved be accommodated?

30. What should be evaluated?

    - The purpose of the event?
    - The design?
    - The implementation?
    - The evaluation process chosen?
    - The totality?

- Or something else?
- Who should decide? When?

31. What should be the order of priority? How quick must the evaluation be?

    - Why that quick?
    - What are the longer-term implications of the event?

32. When should the evaluation be carried out?

    - Continuously throughout the event?
    - At the conclusion?
    - At some other time?

33. Who should be involved in the evaluation?

    - If the learners themselves are not involved, why not?
    - Who else must be considered?

34. What other follow-up should there be?

Conclusion

35. Will those involved be fully aware of *all* their responsibilities (to themselves and others) within the context of this event?

36. Will the event reflect a mature approach to adult learning in which all concerned have the opportunity to experience significant learning through:

    - Self-direction? Self-motivation? Self-development? Self-evaluation?

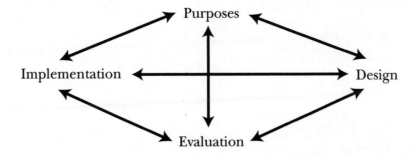

Figure 37.1   The interrelationship between the four main elements of the learning event

37. Will the event also reflect the critical interrelationship between all four main elements as shown in Figure 37.1?

38. Will all learners contribute to all four elements? Will the event be truly learner-centred? Will it really be suitable for *adults*?

Some final thoughts

39. What feelings do these questions arouse in you?

    – Are you encouraged to be reactive? Or proactive?

40. Some would say that any checklist, particularly one which uses words you may not like or appreciate, has a strictly limited usefulness. How do you feel?

41. Having considered the questions, what self-development, if any, do you propose to pursue now?

42. As an adult answering this final question, what are you saying about your own approach to your own learning?

    – Are you satisfied with the answer?

38   Staff development

A prime task of any manager is to help his or her staff develop their capabilities, not only within their current jobs but also in preparation for more senior positions. These capabilities may be extended, in most instances, more effectively in the work environment than by attendance at off-site training courses. The following checklist illustrates a variety of techniques which may be used separately or in combination. Whatever the choice in invidividual cases, however, development plans should be prepared in consultation with each person concerned: possibly during the normal appraisal discussion and periodically thereafter.

1. Do you accept that it is one of your prime management tasks to help your staff develop their job performance?

2. To what extent could the job performance of many, if not all, of your people be improved? How specific can you be? Have you considered in detail their individual strengths? Areas of competence? Areas of possible development? Are these questions considered with them? Or merely about them?

3. Do you personally devote sufficient time *now* to considering the development needs of your staff?

4. When was the last time you carried out an audit of development needs in your department? Would it be worth doing again now?

5. How do you identify the individual development needs of your people? Do you start by considering the main areas of possible development? (See Figure 38.1)

Focus of action	Targets
Remedial	Improving particular aspects of performance which are not up to standard for whatever reason
Developmental	(a) Reinforcing personal strengths (b) Acquiring new skills and knowledge to cope with future work challenges
Creative	(a) Developing better ways of dealing with existing tasks (b) Discovering ways of dealing with new tasks

Figure 38.1   Main areas of possible development

6. Is the situation discussed, and agreement reached, with the person concerned on appropriate development targets?

   – Are the results to be achieved stated clearly?
   – Are specific time frames agreed?

7. How often do these discussions take place with individual staff? Is that often enough?

8. When considering the possible methods of reaching the targets, do you recognize that on-the-job development invariably makes a much more significant contribution to success than off-the-job training courses?

   – What is the balance, both qualitatively and quantitatively, between off-the-job training and on-the-job development activities in your department?
   – Are you satisfied with the answer?

9. Which of the following development activities play a significant role in your department? Which ones could be used more? Or introduced for the first time? What is the balance? Is it acceptable?

   Special assignments/working parties/projects
   – Would special assignments to investigate specific problems for defined periods of time add to the individual's knowledge and experience?
   – How should such assignments be monitored?

Committee assignment
- Would such assignments broaden experience and knowledge, and increase confidence in achieving results by negotiation and discussion? How could such assignments be arranged? Could the individual deputize for you?
- How should progress be monitored?

Coaching and guidance
- Which individuals might benefit particularly from your personal help?
- What help, specifically, is appropriate?
- What pre-planning is necessary?
- How might fruitful discussions be set up? And 'learning contracts' agreed?
- Do you possess the interpersonal skills appropriate to be an effective coach?
- What is your relationship now with the individual(s) concerned? Does a firm base for coaching exist already?
- How should progress be monitored?

Job rotation/secondment
- Would the individual benefit from broadening/updating his or her technical knowledge/experience? Supervisory/management experience?
- How critical is the need?
- Would rotation within the department meet the need? If so, when? For how long?
- If not, could secondment to another department/division be arranged? To a supplier/customer? To some outside agency? Again, when? And for how long?
- In any event, how should progress be monitored?

Study for formal qualifications
- Should the individual be encouraged to study for further technical or professional qualifications?
- What are the possibilities of encouraging the individual to join an organization-based distance learning group?
- How close are your ties with local higher education establishments? Are you aware of the opportunities on offer?
- What monitoring is appropriate?

Membership of professional societies
- Should the individual be encouraged to participate actively in a particular professional society? To stand for office to gain wider administrative/managerial/public relations experience?

- How? When?

Planned delegation
- Which of your present responsibilities/tasks might provide a valuable learning experience for individual members of staff?
- How should these tasks be delegated? Orally? Or in writing?
- To what sort of approach would each individual react best?
- Will all those concerned be made aware of the responsibilities you have delegated?
- Will you leave the individual concerned to get on with the job? Will you also delegate the right to be wrong?
- Will an attitude of 'watchful neglect' be appropriate on your part?
- When the tasks are completed, how will you evaluate the effect of your delegation?

    • On the individual? With the individual?
    • On yourself? (See also Checklist 8.)

Mentoring
- Has the possibility been considered of appointing 'mentors' (i.e. helpers) from amongst your more senior staff to assist in the development of inexperienced staff?
- Which of your more experienced staff might also be helped to develop themselves (development-by-self) by assuming the role of mentor to particular individuals (who would experience development-of-self)?
- If such a possibility has not been considered, should it be? When? Who else should be involved?
- What monitoring would be appropriate?
- If 'mentoring' is an unfamiliar term, what should you do? What will you do?

Planned self-development
- Are individuals actively involved in their own self-development?
- If not, would it be worth while asking everyone to conduct a written personal assessment of their own contribution to departmental efforts? And to prepare subsequently a proposed action plan (similar to Figure 19.7) for discussion with you before implementation is agreed?
- What monitoring of self-development plans takes place currently? Should such monitoring be extended?
- What more could you do to extend the impact of self-development as a staff development tool? What should you do? What will you do? (See also Checklist 36.)

Off-the-job training courses
- If a training course appears to be the most (only?) effective way of meeting a particular development need, how will the most appropriate course be chosen?

  - On reputation?
  - On cost?
  - On availability?
  - Or what?

- Will the individual concerned be fully briefed before the event?
- Will agreement be concluded on

  - Why attendance is considered appropriate?
  - What your expectations are concerning pre-course preparation? On return from the course?

10. What possible development methods not mentioned above could you use to encourage a more critical self-awareness of personal performance standards amongst your staff?

    - How can you encourage them to be more proactive about their learning? How can you help them to develop their approach to on-the-job learning?

11. What action do you intend to take now? What targets do you intend to set yourself? What steps will you take to extend your commitment to helping your people develop themselves?

12. How willing are you to commit yourself to discussing progress every week with at least one member of your staff?

13. How much time will you devote each week to reviewing progress and formulating appropriate action plans? Half-an-hour? An hour? More?

14. How will you monitor your own self-imposed development targets?

39   Succession planning

Ensuring continuity of effort in achieving organizational objectives is a perennial problem for managers at all levels. It involves planning for both the unexpected (resignations, long-term sickness, and more) and the expected (retirements). It does require considerable self-discipline to deal with what may never happen, although it is inevitable that some staff movements will occur. How you deal with both contingencies and the planned development of staff will affect your own managerial reputation.

Current situation

1. What is the present staffing situation in the department(s)/sections(s) for which you are responsible?

    – By department/section?
    – By skill level/occupational category?
    – By wage/salary grade?
    – By age distribution?
    – By length of service?

2. How many staff have resigned in the past twelve months? How many have been dismissed? What is the current absence rate? Is it rising/steady/falling?

3. What does this information about the current staffing situation tell you? What is its impact now on results in your area?

4. What is the current annual cost to the organization of employing these people? Of employing you?

– How much could be saved by making better use of the skills and knowledge of individual staff? Of your own skills and knowledge?

5. How much do you know about the relative strengths of your staff at all levels? Is this a sufficient basis on which to plan their future?

– Does the performance appraisal system indicate which staff are likely to succeed in what jobs in the future?
– Are the recommendations arising from the performance appraisal system being acted on now? Are you sure? How do you know?

  • Who needs training? Or retraining?
  • In what skills?
  • When? Over what time-scale?

– What action do your answers suggest?

6. Which jobs in your area (other than your own) are critical to results? How easy is it for you to answer the following questions with regard to 'key jobs'?

– Job title?
– Current job holder?
– Age?
– Time in job?
– Next job?
– Current development plans?
– Planned replacement?

What are the strengths in your area? What potential problems (possible weaknesses) does your analysis suggest?

Future requirements

7. What will be the effect of the organization's future plans on staffing levels in your department(s)/section(s)?

– Looking forward from today, will more/less/different people and skills be needed? In a year's time? In two years' time? A longer period?
– Which jobs, not currently vital to performance, could become so as a result of these changes? Who could be developed/develop themselves for these jobs? Present job holders? Or others?

Action

8. What are you doing now to ensure that future staffing needs in your area will not cause disruption? Are you genuinely planning ahead? Or are staff crises continually planning you?

9. What additional information concerning your staff do you need to generate/request from others?

    – Do you know *now* who will reach normal retiring age in the next year? The following year? The year after that?
    – Are you clear about who could replace key staff in the event of accident? How ready would they be?
    – Or do you believe in pitching people in at the deep end to see whether they can swim? If so, do you accept readily the responsibility for periodically removing the floating corpses?

      • What could this approach be doing to your professional reputation as a manager?
      • What could it be doing to you as a person?

10. What action are you currently taking to ensure that the fullest use is made, amongst others, of the development methods illustrated below to help individual members of your staff to prepare themselves for the future?

    – Coaching and guidance
    – Special assignments/projects/working parties
    – Committee assignments
    – Job rotation/secondment
    – Study for formal qualifications
    – Planned delegation
    – Mentoring
    – Off-the-job training courses

11. What more could you be doing now? What more could your section heads/supervisors be doing? In what ways particularly do you show by your actions that you consider 'people planning' to be fundamental to future success? Are you really doing enough?

12. For instance, what are you doing now to develop your own successor?

13. Which member of your staff would you choose to assume your own responsibilities if tomorrow, for whatever reason, you were unable to continue?

– Why would you choose this person? Are your values showing through your answer? Or your prejudices? Are you really operating on the basis of equal opportunity for all?

14. Is this person as ready as he or she can be to do the job now?

   – If not, do you accept that you are lessening your chances of moving on if you do not adopt a proactive stance in this respect?

15. What were the results of this person's most recent appraisal?

   – What is your estimate of the individual's performance currently? How big is the gap between ideal and actual performance?
   – What specifically is the cause of this gap?
   – What development action was agreed at the most recent appraisal discussion? Is it happening? When did you last check?

16. What skills need to be developed? What additional knowledge is needed? What attitudes still need to mature?

   – What are the agreed priorities? And the time frames?
   – In which context, principally, will the development take place? On-the-job? Or off-the-job?
   – Can the critical needs be achieved by more committed coaching from you? By delegating new tasks? By using other methods illustrated earlier? Or by using external training courses?

17. Will you discuss these additional development proposals with the person concerned?

   – Will any decisions be made jointly? If not, why not?

18. Is it now worth reviewing questions 13 to 17 for your 'second choice' individual?

19. Do you expect your own immediate staff to adopt the same planned approach to development? Are they quite clear about what you expect? Are you sure?

   – What periodic checks do you make to ensure that what you want to happen does indeed happen?
   – Should such checks be stepped up?
   – How often do you meet with your immediate staff to discuss succession planning? Is that often enough?

20. Are you genuinely in a position to commit to paper your plans for people's movements in your area? Over the next year? The following

year? A longer period? If you cannot, then is it more likely that your area will plan you rather than the reverse?

40   You and your job

This checklist is designed to help you assess the impact both you and others have on your current job within the organization you represent, and to identify the steps you might take to gain added job satisfaction and make the job itself more worthwhile.

1. What sort of work do you do?

    - What particular type(s) of work provide a focus for your activities?
    - In what sort of organization do you work?
    - What is the prevailing culture in your organization?
    - Is the associated management style one of which you approve?
    - To what extent are you comfortable with this style?

2. What impact does your organization's culture and management style have on the work you do? Is the impact wholly positive? Less so? Or is its impact negative?

3. Where does your job, your position, fit into the organization? To whom do you report?

    - Who are your colleagues at the same level in your organization's hierarchy?
    - At what level of responsibility are you operating? How much discretion in decision making do you have?
    - What level(s) of decision(s) are an integral part of your job? Are these decisions primarily strategic? Tactical? Or operational? (See Figure 40.1.)

4. How many people are you responsible for?

    - What tasks do they perform?

Decision level	Discretionary element	Focus	Time frame
Strategic	High	Deciding future directions in an organization-wide context	Long term
Tactical	Moderate	Deciding how strategic decisions should be implemented	Medium term
Operational	Low	Deciding responses to matters of the moment	Short term

Figure 40.1   Levels of decision making

- What sort of people are they?
- Are they fully trained/qualified/experienced for the jobs they are doing? How do you know?

5. What authority does your position involve at the moment? What decisions do you take on the following issues:

- Recruiting and selecting staff?
- Physical resources?
- Budget(s)?
- Other spending?
- Deciding staff merit increases?
- Promoting staff?
- Disciplining/dismissing staff?

6. To what extent do you feel that the authority you have within your position is sufficient for your current role? Is there a genuine balance between your responsibilities and authority?

7. Are you fully aware of all the elements which comprise your role at work now? (See Figure 40.2.)

- What is the relative importance of each of these elements?
- What controls apply to each of the main elements? To your job in total?
- Would it be worth checking your perceptions with those of your boss?

8. Are there any elements of your job which pull you in different directions?

Element (area of responsibility/ accountability). Indicate importance to overall job success (low/ moderate/ high)	Match between responsibilities and authorities (low/ moderate/ high/total)	Degree of conflict (none/low/ moderate/ high)	Ambiguity (none/low/ moderate/ high)	Differing expectations (none/some/ many)
1				
2				
3				
4				
5				
6				
7				
8				
9				
10				

Figure 40.2   The elements of your role

– What could be done to minimize/eradicate such conflict?
– What should be done?
– What can you do personally?

9. Are there any elements of your job which cause you particular concern because different people have varying expectations of their achievement?

– How much ambiguity is present in your role currently?
– What could/should be done to minimize/eradicate such differing expectations? And ambiguity?
– Would it be worth checking your perceptions with your boss? When?

10. Do you possess a written description for your position?

– If so, is it accurate? Clear? Balanced? Up-to-date? Sufficiently flexible? And does it include clear reference to your 'core' responsibilities as a manager?

• When was the last time the description was updated?

- Was the update completed because the formal structure in your organization changed?
- Because the content of your job changed?
- Because you had been appointed to the job?
- Or because inaccuracies had been highlighted?
- Or for other reason(s)? If so, what?

  – If you do not have a description for your position, are you aware of everything which is expected of you? Would a written job description (terms of reference) be beneficial? If so, what should you do? How soon?

11. Do you periodically review your job performance with your own immediate boss as part of a formal appraisal/review process in your organization?

    – Is your performance reviewed against mutually agreed major objectives, clearly expressed in writing?
    – What overall impression did you gain from your boss on the most recent occasion about your performance during the review period?
    – If your performance is reviewed rather more informally, and continues to be reviewed in this way, are you happy with both the method, and the results? Should you be happy with the method? The results?
    – How can you ensure that your boss conducts (even?) more effective reviews against measurable criteria in the future?

      - What should you do? When?

12. What appear to be your main strengths in relation to your performance currently?

    – What are you good at?

      - What does your boss recognize that you are good at?
      - What do other people think?
      - Could there be a difference between what you (and others) think you are good at, and what you genuinely are good at?

    – What are your weaknesses, if any, in relation to your performance? What are you not so good at?

      - What does your boss think in this respect?
      - Are you both in agreement? Or not?
      - What do others think?
      - Again, could there be a difference between what you (and others) think you are good at, and what you really are good at?

- In either case, what are you doing to rectify any shortcomings? Is that sufficient for current circumstances?
- Could you be experiencing difficulty in recognizing any short-comings? What action does your answer suggest?

  • How could you find out?
  • Who could help to clarify the situation?
  • How soon?

13. Having considered your responses to these questions, are you absolutely sure that you are clear about what your organization expects of you in your present position? Or, if not, about the action you should take to clarify the situation? And to reduce/eliminate the impact of any ambiguity? Of any conflict?

14. Which particular elements of your current position enthuse you most? What do you really like doing as part of your job? Which elements enthuse you least? What do you particularly dislike doing?

    - Why, specifically, do you like doing the particular things you have identified? And conversely, why specifically, do you *not* like doing the things you have identified?

Having reflected on your responses, complete Figure 40.3.

'Likes'	'Dislikes'	Reasons?

Figure 40.3   Likes and dislikes

15. To what extent are your 'likes' the result of exercising particular skills?

The result of being with particular people? A reflection of your impact on the organization's activities? Or are there other reasons which explain your 'likes'? Which, particularly?

16. And to what extent are your 'dislikes' the result of *not* exercising, or *not* having, particular skills? The result of working with people who make you feel particularly uncomfortable? Your perception of particular elements of your job, or particular tasks, as being trivial? Or unnecessary? Or are there other reasons? Which, specifically? Now review your responses to questions 6–9 and compare them with your responses to questions 11–16.

17. What is the short-term significance of the responses you have included in Figure 40.3? The longer-term significance?

18. How far currently do you feel that there is insufficient time in a working day to achieve all that is expected of you? That you are suffering from 'overload'?

    – When did you last conduct a thorough review of how you spend your time at work?
    – Would it be worth doing so again, now?
    – Or do you not have the time to spare? Can you/should you conduct such a review anyway if this is the case?
    – As a quick check, how many of the situations illustrated in Figure 40.4 apply to you currently? What other 'time' problems not mentioned there have an impact on your work currently?

• Missing deadlines	• Feeling you have to say 'yes' to people regardless of your commitments
• Putting off things you ought to do	• Waiting in meetings which start late
• Spending too long on telephone calls you did not start	• Achieving less than you think your efforts deserve
• Being less than incisive during telephone calls you did start	• Failing to keep promises on work-related matters
• Being unsure where your time goes	• Having insufficient time to think

Figure 40.4   Common 'time' problems

19. Conversely, do you feel that there is too much time in a working day to meet your organization's expectations? That you are in an 'underload' situation?

   – If so, how do you invest this spare time?

     • Are you making particular efforts to extend your personal skills and knowledge?
     • If you are not using the time for your own self-development, what are you doing with it?
     • Can you justify your action? Or inaction?
     • To whom should you justify it, apart from yourself?

   – Whether you are in an overload, or underload, situation, what skills do you possess which you could use, but do not do so? Why is this?

20. Apart from any analysis and review of your time investment, and any self-development you are undertaking, what other action do your answers to questions 17–19 suggest you should take to accommodate any over- or under-load?

   – How great is the mismatch between your competence and capacity, and your organization's expectations of you?
   – What should be done?
   – How soon?

21. How often do you feel that you are excluded from discussions and other consultations which have a direct or indirect impact on your work?

22. How many decisions have been made about your job and the way in which you do it in the past six months where you found out about the decision only after the event?

23. How many times recently have you expected support from particular people which was not forthcoming? Were your expectations realistic? If so, what happened? Why?

24. Can you recollect feeling that developments in technology, and other changes within the organization, are happening too fast for you to keep up? That you are having to run faster and faster in order to stand still? That you are in ever greater danger of falling behind and becoming out-of-date? How strong is this feeling currently?

25. How often recently have you been exhorted to improve or extend your productivity at work? To achieve more and more, with less and less?

Aspects of your current position and its environment	Action required Yes No	Focus of action (description)	Help needed from . . . ?	Comple-tion by (date)
Current management style				
'Fit' between responsibilities and authority				
Clarity of role				
Written terms of reference (job description)				
Informal understanding				
Degree of conflict				
Degree of ambiguity				
Elements liked/ satisfying				
Elements disliked/ dissatisfying				
Levels of application of personal skills				
Presence of 'overload' (too much to do)				
Presence of 'underload' (too little to do)				
Level of consultation on matters affecting your role				
Level of management support				
Ability to accommodate/ maintain currency in relation to technological and other changes				
Requirement to extend productivity				
Match of personal needs/abilities to requirements of position				

Figure 40.5   Position analysis/action plan

- What do your answers to questions 22–25 tell you about your current perceptions of what you do and how you do it?
- How much stress are you suffering from your continuing efforts to maintain and develop your position?
  - How much more stress can you foresee presenting itself in the next six months?
  - Thereafter?
  - What is actually causing you to be stressed now?
  - What could cause you to be stressed in the future?

26. What, if anything, do you need to do to remove the blockages on your job? On your thought processes in relation to your job? (See Figure 40.5.) On anything in your non-work life which may be blocking your thinking?